A YEAR OF
THE LORD'S FAVOUR

GRACE IN TIMES OF NEED
A MEMOIR

PETE WILCOX

A Year of the Lord's Favour

Church House Publishing
Church House
27 Great Smith Street
London SW1P 3AZ

www.chpublishing.co.uk

ISBN 978 1 78140 508 6 PB
ISBN 978 1 78140 509 3 e-ISBN

Published 2025 by Church House Publishing

Text copyright © Pete Wilcox 2025

All rights reserved. No part of this publication may be reproduced or stored or transmitted by any means or in any form, electronic or mechanical, including photocopying, recording, or any information storage and retrieval system without written permission, which should be sought from: copyright@churchofengland.org

The opinions expressed in this book are those of the contributors and do not necessarily reflect the official policy of the General Synod or The Archbishops' Council of the Church of England.

Scripture quotations (other than from the Psalms) are from the New Revised Standard Version of the Bible, Anglicized Edition, copyright © 1989, 1995 by the Division of Christian Education of the National Council of the Churches of Christ in the USA. Used by permission. All rights reserved.

Material from *Common Worship: Services and Prayers for the Church of England* is copyright © The Archbishops' Council 2000-2008. Prayers from the Methodist Covenant service from *The Methodist Worship Book* are © 1999 Trustees for Methodist Church Purposes.

EU GPSR Authorised Representative
LOGOS EUROPE, 9 rue Nicolas Poussin, 17000, LA ROCHELLE, France
E-mail: Contact@logoseurope.eu

No part of this book may be used or reproduced in any manner for the purpose of training artificial intelligence technologies or systems.

Cover design by www.penguinboy.net
Internal design and typesetting by ForDesign

CONTENTS

Introduction		1
November 2016	Sheffield Calling	5
December 2016	Reset Required	11
January 2017	Seeking Equilibrium	15
February 2017	Letting Go	19
March 2017	Fresh Upheaval	25
April 2017	Unexpected Twists	33
May 2017	Competing Demands	43
June 2017	All Change	51
July 2017	Enduring Treatment	61
August 2017	Welcome Recuperation	69
September 2017	Joyful Celebration	73
October 2017	Settling In	81
November 2017	Undergoing Surgery	85
December 2017	Looking Back	93
	Postscript	96
	Acknowledgements	100

/continued

Presidential address to Sheffield Diocese Synod, November 2022	102
The 2014 House of Bishops' Declaration on the Ministry of Bishops and Priests	110
Statement on the announcement of my appointment, April 2017	113
Sermon preached at the Service of Installation, September 2017	117

INTRODUCTION

This book is my attempt to tell the story of the most tumultuous twelve months of my life. Like the church year, the story begins and ends at the start of Advent: it runs from Sunday 27 November 2016 to Sunday 5 December 2017. It relates how I became both a bishop in the Church of England and (more or less simultaneously) a cancer patient.

There are at least three significant risks associated with my decision to publish a memoir of that year-long experience. The first and most important is that this is not just my story. Plenty of other people are implicated in it, a number of them named in the pages which follow. They include lay and ordained colleagues in the Diocese of Sheffield (where I now serve as bishop) as well as in Liverpool, where I was previously Dean. Many readers will be aware that the early months of the period in question were distressing ones in our Diocese and beyond. I earnestly hope and pray that the publication of this memoir will not re-open old wounds. My sense is that enough time has now elapsed for that risk to be minimal – not least because Philip North has recently been appointed as Bishop of Blackburn, enabling him to draw a line under what was a publicly painful period. Philip has kindly read and graciously welcomed this memoir: without his encouragement I could not have proceeded to publish it.

The second risk is that my account will flatter me – a potential pitfall in any autobiographical writing. I am familiar with my shortcomings and, as the Psalmist said, 'my sin is ever before me'. I am keenly aware of mistakes I made during the period in question, which impacted especially negatively on my nearest and dearest. Writing this account has allowed me to acknowledge the cost of certain choices I made. However, this is a curated account: I've chosen what to include and what to omit. I have made decisions about the amount of soul-bearing I am prepared to do. While I quote often from my prayer journal, I don't quote everything. My wife Cathy tells me the result is 'sanitised', without some of the rawness we both felt at the time. I also realise that where medical matters are concerned, the point is probably soon reached where 'some information' becomes 'too much information'.

The third risk is that I will inadvertently glorify the experience of surviving cancer. Cancer remains a deeply threatening disease with no very obvious pattern to the outcome. Neither Christian faith nor individual fighting spirit seem to be decisive. Much more significant is the form of cancer, where and how aggressive it is, and the degree of access to medical treatment. Cathy and I mourn the loss of half a dozen friends who have died from cancer. We know that my survival has been something beyond our control.

I was persuaded that these risks are worth taking after delivering a presidential address to the Diocesan Synod in Sheffield. It was in November 2022, a few weeks after I had been discharged by the colorectal department of the Northern General Hospital. I was five years on from surgery to remove a tumour from my colon, and no longer meaningfully at risk of a recurrence of the disease. It was in that address (reproduced at the end of this book on page 102) that I first 'went public' about my experience and put an outline of the story on record, including the fact that I now live with a permanent colostomy. Perhaps predictably, the address provoked much sympathy. More surprising was the fact it also provoked gratitude and appreciation, not least from people who have had to cope with similar challenges.

I drafted this memoir during a period of sabbatical leave in the early months of 2024. As it happens, King Charles III and then the Princess of Wales chose to disclose their own current treatment for unspecified cancers during this period. I was interested to note that their openness about their respective situations was met with that same combination of sympathy and thankfulness. My hope is that this longer, more reflective, memoir might be helpful too.

Specifically, I hope this account will encourage any readers who happen at present to be receiving treatment for cancer. More generally, I hope it might give hope to those who are seeking to follow Jesus faithfully, but who find that they are presented with challenges they would not have chosen. There is a stubborn misconception that for truly faithful followers of Christ Jesus, rough places are consistently made smooth, crooked roads are invariably made straight. That has not been my experience. I hope this account will hearten other believers who find themselves facing sore trials, despite making every effort to walk in the Way. Of course, I hope the book will be of interest to readers beyond these two particular groups – not least because the year in question included some moments of sheer comedy. I hope that here and there this account will bring a smile to readers' faces.

In that address of November 2022, I noted that the illness made me acutely aware of my dependence on others. This has remained formative for me. For all my obvious privilege, I am not a self-sufficient person and the timing of the illness made me determined not to be, or even appear to be, a self-sufficient bishop. Secondly, I observed that the illness made me freshly aware of my mortality, more determined to make the most of each day and to live each day 'unto the LORD'. It was in that sense I concluded my address by saying that the experience of diagnosis and treatment, surgery and recovery had been 'good for me'. I am seeking to expand on that testimony here and to bear witness anew to the grace and kindness of God. I genuinely experienced that twelve-month period, to echo the words of the prophet Isaiah, as 'a year of the LORD's favour'.

Pete Wilcox, Lent 2024

November 2016

SHEFFIELD CALLING

By the summer of 2016, I had been active in ordained ministry for nearly 30 years. I was ordained as a deacon in 1987 and as a priest in 1988, both times by Bishop David Jenkins in Durham Cathedral. Over the course of those three decades, I repeatedly had a very clear sense of the next thing to which God was calling me – and again and again, I was wrong.

When my training was ending and I was preparing to leave theological college to embark on ordained ministry, I was confident I would stay in Cambridge, to combine a curacy with further study for a doctorate at the University. I was so sure this was my calling that I tried very hard to engineer the outcome, and failed. Instead, I served a gloriously ordinary and thoroughly worthwhile curacy on Teesside. This sort of misplaced confidence became something of a pattern over the years: a particular prospect would commend itself to me as the obvious will of God and I would eagerly move towards it, only to discover that the Lord had something quite different in mind.

For example: in 2011, after I had been serving as Canon Chancellor at Lichfield Cathedral for five years, I found myself gravitating towards the likelihood that the Lord might be calling me to be either a suffragan bishop or the principal of a theological college. So it was out of the blue that I received a letter from the Archbishops' Appointments Secretary, inviting me to apply for the post of Dean of Liverpool. I remember marching furiously through the house to find Cathy, brandishing the letter at her and saying, 'I can't believe anyone would think I have the slightest interest in becoming a Dean!' In fact, the five years I went on to serve as Dean of Liverpool were among the most fruitful and fun I have known. I now thank God wholeheartedly for calling me there.

The one exception to this rule of being consistently wrong in my sense of future vocation, was when the See of Sheffield became vacant in mid-2016. I had a profound sense that God was calling me to be the next Bishop of Sheffield. What I could not foresee was how tortuous the journey would be to respond to this calling.

I had been Dean of Liverpool since September 2012, a little over four years. I was at full stretch in the role. However, blessed with an outstanding team of colleagues, lay and ordained, I was finding the experience genuinely fulfilling – exciting even. Congregations were growing, new developments were blossoming, and a major fundraising project appeared to be gaining good traction. And yet I had begun to sense I might not remain there much longer. I had, in fact, been interviewed for a role as a diocesan bishop earlier that year, but was not nominated for that post. When the process began to discern who might be the next Bishop of Sheffield, I found myself very strongly drawn to it. For most of my ordained ministry, I have served in the Northern Province and in urban settings, and I could see an initial 'fit' to a Diocese like Sheffield. Then when the Statement of Need (role description) was produced, and I was able to see more specifically what this ministry would require at this time, I had a clear sense of calling to the role. At the beginning of November 2016 I was delighted to discover that I had been shortlisted for interview.

The interviews were scheduled for the end of the month, on Monday 28th and Tuesday 29th – in my case, on the Monday afternoon. From my point of view, it wasn't ideal that it followed so closely after Advent

Sunday, which fell on 27th November that year. In most cathedrals, Advent Sunday is one of the great days in the liturgical calendar, and Liverpool is no exception. In particular, a wonderful service called 'Darkness into Light' takes place each year on Advent Sunday evening, rehearsing the whole Christian story of salvation and anticipating the coming of God's kingdom. In Liverpool, the service attracts a congregation of many hundreds, drawn to hear the choir sing the Advent anthems, receive the Word of the Lord through the readings from Scripture, and savour the dramatic candlelit processions. That year the service was preceded by an important fundraising reception at which I was due to make an appeal to potential donors.

Preparing adequately for both the fundraising reception and the interview the following day was difficult. So once Advent Sunday was behind me, it was a relief to be able to focus fully on Sheffield.

Travelling to York by train on the day of the interview, I remember feeling quite hopeful, though also apprehensive. My nervousness grew in the taxi to Bishopsthorpe Palace, the official residence of the Archbishop of York and the venue for the interview, and again as I sat in a waiting room somewhat beyond the scheduled start time.

I am a reflective thinker and historically I haven't always performed very well at interview. I don't think on my feet as nimbly as some people and my mind tends to turn over multiple answers to questions, which can make me appear tentative and hesitant. And the Crown Nominations Commission (CNC) is, to me at least, quite an intimidating interviewing body.

Chaired by one or other of the Archbishops (in this case Sentamu, then the Archbishop of York), the CNC consists of 14 voting members and 2 non-voting observers. The voting members are the 2 Archbishops (though sometimes, as in this case, with a diocesan bishop to represent one or other of them); 6 so-called 'central members' elected by the Church of England's General Synod; and 6 members representing the particular Diocese involved. The observers are the Archbishops' Appointments Secretary and the Prime Minister's Appointments Secretary.

This large group was seated in an arc, in a spacious reception room. The interview was quite a formal process. Each candidate was expected to preach on the Gospel reading set for that day, and to give a presentation on a set topic. Those two exercises were followed by a formidable period of interrogation. I didn't know at the time how many candidates in all had been called to interview, though I assumed it was two on the Monday (of whom I was one), and two more on the Tuesday.

My interview lasted about 90 minutes in all. Travelling home to Liverpool afterwards, I was reasonably content. Of course, I knew that I could have answered some of the questions more effectively, and was aware that I had rather rushed and garbled my presentation. But I was confident about the homily I had delivered, and on balance felt I had given the panel a sufficient insight into the sort of bishop I might be.

The next day was a long one. Interviews continued at Bishopthorpe in the morning, while I tried unsuccessfully to focus on various tasks back in Liverpool. I knew the CNC would move into 'discernment mode' in the afternoon, seeking to reach a common mind about the person called by God to take up this role. Inevitably, I became more anxious and despondent as the afternoon wore on and evening came. My assumption was that the first person to hear the outcome of the process would be the preferred candidate and that the later it got, the less likely it was that that person would be me.

So it proved. Eventually, after 8.30pm, Archbishop Sentamu phoned to let me know that the CNC's discernment process had led the members to nominate one of the other candidates. It would be many weeks before I discovered who that was.

Over the phone, Archbishop Sentamu said some kind things about my interview. In particular, he stressed that I was the CNC's 'second candidate'. For historic reasons, the CNC is (or at least was) required to present to the Prime Minister two names, not one only; by convention the Prime Minister duly nominates the first name to the Sovereign. So, while I was grateful to the Archbishop for letting me know I was the second candidate, I told him I took that to be a formality only.

'Not always,' he replied.

I remember registering that as a slightly curious thing for him to say. Nonetheless, the following morning in my prayer journal, I simply noted, 'OK, as you were: no Bishop of Sheffield for me. Help me, O God, to embrace this as your good will and purpose for me and as the gift of your providence.' I was forced to conclude that the pattern of my misplaced confidence about where the Lord was calling me was repeating itself.

The following day, the last day of November, I took a second phonecall. This one was from the Archbishops' Appointments Secretary. She was at pains to check that the Archbishop had told me that I was the 'second name'.

'Yes,' I replied, 'but I know that's just a formality.'

'It's not always,' she said.

The fact that she used exactly the same words as the Archbishop unsettled me. It was the first hint I had that the process might not be concluded so quickly after all.

Reflecting in my journal, I wrote, 'There is something deeply odd going on, I think, and it remains possible that I will yet be offered the job.'

December 2016

RESET REQUIRED

I spent the next few days feeling unsettled and a little sorry for myself. At that time, it was Archbishop Sentamu's custom to gather the deans of all the cathedrals of the Northern Province for an annual Advent retreat. In 2016 it took place the very next weekend at Whalley Abbey, a retreat house in the Diocese of Blackburn. I remember finding it hard to achieve any sense of stillness or peace at any point during those two days.

On the Saturday I had taken myself off to the chapel for some solitude, in search of the presence of God. While I sat there, Archbishop Sentamu came in to join me. I don't know if he went to the chapel for his own benefit or in search of me. But when he saw me there, he came and sat with me. Obviously, he was and has remained bound by the strict confidentiality which the CNC process requires, but he did say some further reassuring things about his assessment of my vocation to be a bishop. Then, as he left, he added, 'I wonder if the Holy Spirit has fully spoken on this matter yet.'

I didn't know what to make of that, but it fuelled my intuition that there was something peculiar about the situation. It caused me to write in my journal the following morning, 'I pray for this other person, who is presumably in some distress about it, to make a good and right decision and I pray for grace for myself, to hold all this lightly in the next months.'

The first part of that prayer might indeed have been answered positively enough, eventually. The second certainly wasn't.

On Monday 5 December, I wrote in my journal, 'O Lord it's going to take me a while to bounce back from this disappointment – and perhaps I can't, so long as the Sheffield door is even slightly ajar.'

When I had interviewed for a diocesan bishop post the first time, earlier in the year, I had been able to accept the outcome without so much as a backward glance. There was no great heart-searching involved: it was entirely straightforward for me to re-engage with my ministry as the Dean of Liverpool. It felt different this time. By the Tuesday, one week on from the interview, I had begun making daily use of the Methodist Covenant Prayer – a wonderful prayer of rededication and recommitment to God which Methodists use particularly as part of their annual New Year Covenant Service.

> Christ has many services to be done: some are easy,
>   others are difficult;
> some bring honour, others bring reproach;
> some are suitable to our natural inclinations and material interests,
> others are contrary to both;
> in some we may please Christ and please ourselves;
> in others we cannot please Christ except by denying ourselves.
> Yet the power to do all these things is given to us in Christ,
>   who strengthens us.
>
>> I am no longer my own but yours.
>> Put me to what you will, rank me with whom you will;
>> put me to doing, put me to suffering;
>> let me be employed for you or laid aside for you,
>> exalted for you or brought low for you;
>> let me be full, let me be empty,
>> let me have all things, let me have nothing;

> I freely and wholeheartedly yield all things to your pleasure
> and disposal.
> And now, glorious and blessed God, Father, Son and
>   Holy Spirit,
> you are mine and I am yours. So be it.
> And the covenant now made on earth, let it be ratified in
>   heaven. Amen.

I know the prayer isn't to everyone's liking: some understandably find the words 'put me to suffering' problematic. But the overall sense, of fresh resignation to the good will and purpose of God, proved invaluable to me over the following weeks.

What I had suspected was confirmed for me by the Archbishops' Appointments Secretary that week: the person nominated to be the next Bishop of Sheffield was finding it difficult to discern the will of God and had not yet accepted the calling. 'I hope we will know more this week,' she told me. As it happens, it was the following week, on the very day I had travelled to London to meet her for a fuller debrief about my interview, that she gave me the news: the other person had now agreed to let their name go forward. 'I know you must be disappointed,' she said. 'I know how strongly you felt called to the role.'

Advent is traditionally a good time for a stock-taking of the soul and for a bit of a spiritual reset. I gave myself over to that task for the rest of December. The rhythm of Advent worship, especially in a cathedral and, I dare say, especially in Liverpool, provides much nourishment for the soul. Liverpool Cathedral is the largest cathedral in England, the largest Anglican Cathedral in the world, and that makes it a huge canvas on which to paint Advent. Traditionally, the

Advent wreath on the Great West Door and the Christmas tree at the east end of the nave are enormous and extremely powerful symbolically. There are bespoke liturgies like the Holly Bough Service which are designed specifically to harness the potential of the Great Space as a vehicle to convey the joyful hope of Advent. There was every reason for me to suppose that a reset would be effective here.

In addition, our second son had returned briefly from a stint of missionary work in Japan with the organisation Youth With a Mission (YWAM), to introduce us to his new girlfriend. They had met in Tokyo, where she was also working with YWAM, though she is in fact an American from Santa Fe, New Mexico. Our son Tom had no sooner waved her off to spend Christmas with her parents than he told us about his intention to propose to her when he joined her there. We had at least one very real reason for joyful celebration.

Still, my prayer journal that month is littered with sentences like these: 'I'm feeling the pain of Sheffield and I'm struggling to relinquish it somehow'; 'I am still pretty downcast about it all, O God, and in need of your help'; 'Yesterday I did manage to get in touch with some anger over the Sheffield appointment process. This morning it's still there and I reckon I've got some soul-work to do'; 'Bleurgh... I'm not in the happiest period of my life at present. My heart remains heavy, O God.'

January 2017

SEEKING EQUILIBRIUM

The new year was another gilt-edged opportunity for me, psychologically, to draw a line under Sheffield and to move on. That process would, so I thought, be helped by two substantial speaking engagements in my diary.

The first involved a trip to Auschwitz-Birkenau. I had been invited to provide a pair of biblical reflections for a cohort of participants on the Church of England's Strategic Leadership Development Programme, as part of their three-day retreat visit to the former concentration camps in Poland. I was determined to offer my very best work. Obviously, the Holocaust is a disaster on such a scale that it puts minor distresses into perspective. That was helpful to me.

The trip was scheduled for Monday 9 to Thursday 12 January, so I spent much of the first week of the new year drafting my contributions: one exposition of the Old Testament Book of Lamentations, and another of the New Testament Book of Revelation. I hoped the first might help us to reflect on the cry of those who suffer violence, and the second on the fate of those who perpetrate violence.

The faithful and close exposition and interpretation of the Bible is my passion. The opportunity to expound whole books of the Bible at a single sitting is sheer bliss to me. I delight especially in how biblical literature is crafted, and few things give me such joy as to immerse myself in Bible study, in the hope that I can assist others to see that while Holy Scripture is always more than carefully crafted literature, it is seldom less than that. So, it was a blessed diversion for me, and a restorative one, to be able to throw myself into the task as 2017 got underway.

That visit was also undeniably timely in shaking me out of a lingering sense of self-pity. It was my second trip to Auschwitz-Birkenau. The first had been the previous August, as part of the preparation for this visit. On that occasion, the blistering heat forced me to reflect on what it must have been like for prisoners doing slave labour, without adequate shelter or water, when temperatures rose above 30 degrees. It was even more sobering to be there in January. Our visit coincided with snow, and our guided tour of the site took place in sub-zero temperatures. Though we were all wrapped up in winter clothing, by the end of our exploration of the camp most of us were blue with cold and grateful to be able to return to the warmth of our accommodation, mindful that camp inmates had no such respite. It goes without saying that the horrors of Auschwitz-Birkenau defy any attempt to speak adequately of them. As such, though I was grateful for the opportunity I had been given to address the cohort, I did grasp that my task was to help participants to revisit Scripture in the light of Auschwitz-Birkenau, rather than to attempt to make sense of Auschwitz-Birkenau in the light of Scripture.

The second speaking invitation was from the Archdeacons' Conference meeting at Swanwick in Derbyshire towards the end of the month. They had asked me to offer some biblical reflections on contemporary culture, and I chose to offer a reading of the Book of Esther entitled 'Open to God in a turbulent world'. We were still in the first months of the 2017 Trump administration in the USA; I wasn't finding it difficult to make comparisons with King Ahasuerus (also known in some versions of the Bible as Xerxes). Again, I was grateful for the distraction involved in the preparation and delivery of the material – though of course among the archdeacons were those from Sheffield, and one other who had been on the CNC, so as a piece of escapism from my mood of disappointment, it wasn't total.

Towards the end of the month, we heard the delightful news that our son Tom had become engaged to Rosa. They announced their hope to be married in Santa Fe on 31 August, with a possible Service of Wedding Blessing in the Lady Chapel at Liverpool Cathedral in September, for all the many friends and family who would not be able to make the trip to the USA.

As the weeks of January passed, I knew that the day must be approaching when an announcement would be made about an appointment to Sheffield. My journal entry for the last day of January reads: 'I'm still struggling to let go of Sheffield and an announcement must be due pretty soon. The chief casualty, if I'm not careful, could be my sense of trust in your providence O God – so I really do need the quiet day which is scheduled for tomorrow.'

In fact, an announcement was made that very day: the next Bishop of Sheffield was to be Philip North, at that time the Bishop of Burnley. I had known Philip for over a decade. A prominent and charismatic member of the traditionalist catholic strand of the Church of England, Philip is also a wonderfully dedicated disciple of the Lord Jesus, a gifted evangelist and a passionate advocate of our most deprived communities. So, while I certainly did struggle for some days after the announcement with a renewed sense of my own loss, it was genuinely easy for me to welcome his appointment – I was truly pleased. Naive as it may sound, it really did not occur to me on that day that Philip's well-known traditionalist catholic theological convictions about the ordination of women as priests and bishops would prove so controversial.

February 2017

LETTING GO

In light of the announcement of Bishop Philip's appointment, I noted in my prayer journal on 1 February: 'I might now be able to move on from Sheffield. I hope so.'

However, in my expectation that his nomination would be well received in Sheffield and beyond, I was wrong – and far from alone in my misjudgement. But I said at the time that his nomination as Bishop of Sheffield was within a whisker of being genius. This relates to the struggle within the Church of England over recent decades to enable the ordination of women as priests and bishops, particularly the way this has played out in the Diocese of Sheffield. Some of the explanation offered in the next few pages is quite technical – the only section of the memoir in which I have felt it necessary to resort to footnotes. Some readers may wish to skip over it because they are already perfectly familiar with this piece of the Church of England's recent history. Others may wish to do so because they are complete strangers to it!

When I trained for ordained ministry in the late 1980s, only a handful of my fellow students were female. At that time, it was not possible for women to be ordained as priests – only as deacons. Indeed, the year I was ordained as a deacon (1987), was the first year even that had been possible for women in the Church of England. In the C of E, every new member of the clergy is first ordained as a deacon (which means something like 'servant'). Some people know themselves called to be permanent deacons (known as distinctive deacons) and serve gloriously in that capacity for years. But for most clergy, the diaconate is a one-year period of preparation for further ordination as a priest.

In the late 1980s and early 1990s there was a group of women who were ordained as deacons, but who sensed that they were called to be priests. They had the distressing experience of being ordained to the diaconate alongside male peers one year, but the next being forced to watch when those male peers were ordained as priests, whilst they were not permitted.

It was in 1992 that the General Synod finally voted to allow women to be ordained as priests, and the first such ordinations took place in 1994. At that time I was a vicar in Gateshead in the Durham diocese and I recall my joy at attending one of the two services in Durham Cathedral dedicated to the ordination of women as priests. This year we have just celebrated the 30th anniversary of that significant milestone.

It was another 20 years before the Church of England enabled the ordination of women as bishops. The step required a 'Declaration on the Ministry of Bishops and Priests' from the House of Bishops, made in May 2014. Central to the declaration are the Five Guiding Principles, first commended by the House of Bishops in 2013 (reproduced at the back of this book on page 111). These attempt to affirm both that 'the Church of England is fully and unequivocally committed to all orders of ministry being open equally to all, without reference to gender' and that 'the Church of England remains committed to enabling [those… who, on grounds of theological conviction, are unable to receive the ministry of women bishops or priests] to flourish within its life and structures.'

Alongside these principles, the declaration set out arrangements to enable the continued flourishing of 'those whose theological conviction leads them to seek the priestly or episcopal ministry of men'. Under these arrangements, it was agreed that a Parochial Church Council (PCC) could petition the Diocesan Bishop to seek episcopal oversight from a (male) bishop who shares the theological convictions of the

PCC. For shorthand, these arrangements have become known as 'extended episcopal oversight'.

The point of all this is that as a traditionalist catholic, Bishop Philip is precisely 'one of those who on grounds of theological conviction, [is] unable to receive the ministry of women bishops or priests'. The reason why it seemed to me that his nomination to the See of Sheffield was potentially inspired is that the Diocese of Sheffield has, I am told, the highest proportion of parishes under extended episcopal oversight outside the Diocese of London.

In 2017, there were a total of 175 parishes in the Diocese of Sheffield. Of these, 26 had successfully petitioned for extended episcopal oversight. The majority of these PCCs (21) had done so out of traditionalist catholic theological convictions and were receiving the episcopal ministry of the Bishop of Beverley. A further 5 had done so out of complementarian evangelical convictions and were receiving the episcopal ministry of the Bishop of Maidstone. (A complementarian evangelical holds the conviction that, according to the scriptures, men and women have equal, but complementary roles, and that the role of local church leadership is reserved to men.) Many dioceses with more parishes have far fewer under extended episcopal oversight. I was among those who hoped that Philip North's appointment would provide great reassurance to this significant minority of parishes in the Diocese of Sheffield, while still being a source of encouragement to the majority of parishes who welcomed women priests and bishops. In 2017 women made up almost a quarter of stipendiary incumbents in the Diocese of Sheffield (as well as the majority of self-supporting clergy) and many of the male clergy were ardent supporters of their female colleagues. I am a firm advocate of the ordination of women myself.

However, my confidence that Bishop Philip's nomination would be well received was misplaced. This is not the place to attempt to review why events unfolded over the course of the ensuing weeks in the way that they did. Readers who wish to revisit that process may wish to consult the independent review conducted by Sir Philip Mawer, published in September 2017. The Mawer report is readily available online and part 3 provides a detailed narrative of events.*

The report makes it clear that misgivings about Philip's appointment were being expressed within a week of the announcement, not least at a gathering of female clergy convened at his request at Doncaster Minster on 7 February. I was entirely unaware of any rumblings until around a fortnight later.

At this point, I was still making daily use of the Methodist Covenant Prayer, still unable to let go of a sense of my vocation to Sheffield, still unable to re-engage fully with my role as Dean of Liverpool, which had until now been so rewarding. In the first three weeks of the month, my prayer journal is full of wrestlings of my own: 'I'm downhearted, on account of the continued sorrow I feel about Sheffield' (2nd); 'my sense of loss over Sheffield isn't dissipating really' (13th); 'My heart remains heavy over Sheffield' (16th); 'I'm still not reconciled to what happened' (19th); and 'I woke up again this morning thinking of Sheffield and what's not to be' (21st).

Meanwhile, there was a speaking engagement in my diary which required a good deal of preparation in February. It was an opportunity for me to offer, once again, some sustained exposition of the Bible. But where I would usually have relished the hours spent in preparation, on this occasion it was complicated.

---

* See https://www.churchofengland.org/media/press-releases/independent-reviewers-report-see-sheffield-published.

✧

Two years before, Steven Croft (then the Bishop of Sheffield), had invited me to speak at a 'Leading Well' retreat to be held at Scargill House in Yorkshire in early March 2017. The attendees at the gathering were to be new and newish incumbents from Sheffield Diocese. In 2015, Sheffield had no particular resonance for me as I was entirely focused on my ministry in Liverpool. But Scargill House is a beautiful place, Steven was someone I held in high regard, and the retreat was far enough ahead to mean space could be found in my diary. So I had gladly agreed.

Of course, the prospect of that retreat shifted in significance for me as soon as I was shortlisted for interview. Back then I had reflected that in March I would either be meeting part of my new flock, or would be confronted with an acute reminder of what might have been. Towards the end of February 2017, it appeared to be very much the latter. As the engagement drew nearer, the last thing I wanted was to spend three days with clergy from the Diocese of Sheffield of all places. As such, the preparation for the retreat, instead of being a blissful escape, became a real challenge, which required me to dig deep.

At the same time, the furore over Philip's nomination was becoming a matter of national interest. Key civic voices in Sheffield, including local politicians, were drawn into the debate and were questioning the wisdom of the nomination. Then on Friday 24 February, Professor Martyn Percy published an article on the Modern Church website, openly critical of Philip's nomination and calling on him 'to reflect on his position'. At that point Martyn Percy was Dean of Christ Church, Oxford; he and his wife Emma had both previously served as a licensed priests in Sheffield. The following day the article received considerably greater attention when Professor Percy followed it up with a piece in The Guardian. As the Mawer report puts it, 'the effect of Professor

Percy's article and the report of it in The Guardian was to elevate what had previously been essentially a matter of controversy within the Diocese of Sheffield to that of a story of regional and national significance.'

I later discovered that Philip began a period of retreat, precisely to reflect on his position, on 28 February. I was blissfully unaware of this at that time, writing in my journal on 27 February, 'The Philip North furore sounds as if it has blown over. Women who have served with Philip speak very highly of him. So that, I suspect, is that.'

And on 28 February, which was Shrove Tuesday (the eve of Lent), I wrote, 'I continue to struggle with the whole Sheffield thing. My Lenten task will be to let it go.'

Not for the first time, I was entirely wrong.

March 2017

FRESH UPHEAVAL

On 1 March, Ash Wednesday, I was in a suitably Lenten mood. I noted in my journal, 'I'm really finding it very difficult to get over Sheffield and past it.' But in fact, in the next few days I experienced what seemed at the time to be a very positive shift in my perspective.

Years before, in 2010, when I was a residentiary canon in Lichfield, I had suffered a bout of labyrinthitis, which left me with permanent tinnitus. To this day, I have a constant ringing in my ears. To begin with I found the noise extremely intrusive, especially at the end of the day, when it made it particularly difficult for me to fall asleep. Initially I desperately hoped that at some point the condition would disappear. Indeed, the medical advice was that it might. But quite quickly I decided that it would be better for my peace of mind if I did not pin my hopes on relief, but sought instead to adjust to the noise as a permanent fact of life. I stopped hoping I would get over the tinnitus, and sought rather to live with it. Very soon, I found I had adapted: if at any moment I stopped to register it, I found the noise had not gone away – it was ever-present; but most days I barely noticed it at all.

In early Lent 2017, a penny seemed to drop, and I remember saying to Cathy: 'I think I need to approach the Sheffield thing in the way that I approached the tinnitus. Instead of hoping the sense of loss will go away, I think I just have to learn to live with it. I think I might have to reconcile myself to the fact that I will never be reconciled to what has happened.' That psychological move felt like to me a genuine breakthrough at the time. It certainly helped me to enter into the Leading Well retreat in a calmer frame of mind.

The retreat took place between Tuesday 7 and Thursday 9 March. It involved almost 40 clergy from the Diocese of Sheffield – a very significant proportion of the entire cohort of stipendiary incumbents. Inevitably, the atmosphere was tense. The ongoing controversy in the Diocese had featured on BBC Radio 4's Sunday programme on 5 March, and it was widely reported on Monday 6th that Philip had entered into a period of retreat himself.

That felt like an ominous development. For the first time, it seemed to me possible that Philip might indeed withdraw his nomination. In my journal I wrote, 'I guess that if Philip does withdraw, it will be necessary to run the whole CNC process again, and I shall have to consider whether or not to allow my name to go forward for that, since it might be just too much for me to take a further knock back. But that is to get ahead of myself. Suffice to say that, three months later, the situation is evidently still not done and dusted.'

I don't remember very much about the first afternoon of the retreat. I do remember that Peter Burrows, the Bishop of Doncaster and Acting Bishop of Sheffield, had not turned up at Scargill, although I had been assured he would be there. I realised that was because, at a moment of great uncertainty, it was necessary for him to remain present in the diocese. I had decided to offer a series of reflections on passages from the life of Moses in Exodus 1 to 18, and I recall how poignant it was, in that particular context, to begin in the opening session by reflecting on the vital role and leadership of two women, the midwives Shiphrah and Puah in Exodus 1.

That evening, life took a very unexpected and drastic turn. The first hint was when I took a phonecall from a member of staff in the National Church Institutions. Unusually, he greeted me as Peter. He knows full well that I strongly prefer to be Pete, but I took it to be a small aberration. But then he said, 'Caroline [meaning Caroline Boddington, the Archbishops' Appointments Secretary] tells me you'd like a bit of help with your statement?'

That made no sense at all to me. 'No,' I replied, 'I've not spoken to Caroline.'

There was a long pause at the other end, after which, calmly, but undeniably abruptly, he said, 'Ok, thanks. Bye.'

My immediate assumption was that he had been trying to call Peter Burrows, the Bishop of Doncaster, and had called me by excruciating mistake. I later discovered that he had in fact called me in the mistaken belief that I had already been informed by Caroline of unfolding events, but that she had been unable to reach me. In any event, the brief exchange left me in no doubt that Philip had decided to withdraw from the process. However, I was entirely unclear what the implications of that might be.

Scargill House is set in the Yorkshire Dales, outside the village of Kettlewell. One of its special beauties is its remote countryside location But a consequence is that a phone signal can sometimes be elusive there. As a result, on that Tuesday evening I missed a series of voicemail messages from Archbishop Sentamu. They were very brief, each one simply asking me to phone him urgently – but they became successively more impatient.

'Pete, this is Sentamu. Please call me.'

'Pete, I need to speak to you. Please call me at once.'

'Wilcox, where are you? Why have you not called me?'

These messages pinged onto my phone in rapid succession at 11.20pm. The brief phonecall I had received earlier in the evening meant that my mind was already in turmoil and I was unable to sleep. In this fractious state, I heard the voicemail notifications come in and listened to them at once. The inevitable result was a wakeful night.

In my sleeplessness, I identified two possibilities. It seemed to me that only two things were realistic. Either this was a pastoral call from Sentamu, simply to let me know about Philip's decision ahead of a press announcement, and to clarify that the CNC process would have to be run again. Or it must be to check on my own sense of calling to Sheffield. I had no way of weighing the relative likelihood of the two options.

Early the next morning, I wrote in my journal, 'How very weird that this this news [of Philip's decision to withdraw] should break – assuming it does today – while I am here at Scargill with so many clergy from Sheffield. Spooky.'

In fact, it would be another 24 hours before the announcement came. But after breakfast and before the next session of the retreat, I managed to return Sentamu's phonecalls from the night before. This required me to walk around the grounds of Scargill in search of a phone signal, as if I was dowsing for water. I eventually found one in a suitably secluded spot and was able to call. I happened to catch the Archbishop while he was at King's Cross Station in London, boarding a train to York. 'Wait one moment,' he told me, 'I need to find a toilet...'

It was from the privacy of a loo on a stationary train that Sentamu confirmed to me that Philip had decided to withdraw. 'Do you still feel called to Sheffield?' he asked me. It was probably the simplest vocational question I have ever been asked, and when I said 'Yes,' he asked if I was prepared to accept the See. Again, immediately, I said 'Yes.' It is the only time in almost 40 years of married life that I have accepted an appointment without consulting for even a moment with Cathy!

'Good,' said Sentamu. And then, with inimitable mischief, and perfect comic timing, 'Now I am going to flush.'

✧

In my journal later that day I noted, 'What an extraordinary few months. But I really could not shake off the sense that this was my calling. And to be here, with these folk who are my future flock – astonishing.'

There was inevitably something surreal about the remainder of the retreat. Through the Wednesday and into Thursday morning, when I was delivering material in plenary, and when I was engaged in conversations with clergy over mealtimes and one-to-one, I could not give off any hint of what I knew. I managed to speak to Cathy on the Wednesday morning, to alert her to the situation. She excused herself from a meeting at work to take my call, and then had to return to the business and behave as if the phonecall she had just taken was entirely routine. She recounts that she barely contributed another word.

Philip's news duly broke on the Thursday afternoon, very soon after the retreat disbanded. I knew how distressed he must be and remember hoping that the media spotlight would quickly focus elsewhere, to give him time and space in which to recover. For myself, I was now bound by the confidentiality of the CNC and was unable to share my own news with anyone, except the Bishop of Liverpool, Paul Bayes. But in the following days, things moved forward swiftly.

On Wednesday 15th, just a week after my phonecall with Sentamu, I was in London for a medical appointment with various tests at a Harley Street clinic in the morning, and for a follow up with Dr Angus Blair in the afternoon. He told me that my liver, kidneys and heart were all fine, but that my prostate-specific antigen (PSA) score was very high, for which he recommended a follow up. Afterwards, in my journal, I wrote: 'It could be prostate cancer, could be something else. I discover I'm not actually anxious however.' I think the reason I wasn't anxious was that I had felt so strongly guided by God in the previous months – but I was wrong if I thought that meant there was no problem here.

In between those appointments came a briefing meeting with Caroline Boddington, to work out a possible timeline for announcement and to schedule various other pieces of induction.

Two follow-up scans were arranged for the following week, Thursday 23rd: an MRI scan of my prostate and a CT scan of my heart. Early in the week after that, Dr Blair called to let me know that the CT scan was fine, but that the MRI had shown up some puzzling features 'with possible implications for the bowel'. Further investigation would be wise, he suggested, but he told me he thought sinister outcomes were 'low risk', and that he had assured Caroline Boddington that an announcement of my appointment could go ahead. We began to plan towards Friday 7 April, about two weeks away.

But just as I began to relax into that prospect, there was another unwelcome twist in the saga. At 5pm on Tuesday 28th, my PA took a phonecall from a member of the National Safeguarding Team (NST), asking to speak to me. Puzzled, I took the call. Could she please come to see me, she asked – tomorrow? I inquired if she could tell me what it was she wished to see me about but she couldn't say. I asked if it would be wise for me to be accompanied to the meeting. To my relief she replied 'No.'

Nevertheless, I felt like I had been punched in the solar plexus. I realised it could be something reasonably neutral – she might need to brief me about a safeguarding issue in Sheffield, for example. But the timing, and the urgency, and her unwillingness to elaborate on the phone definitely had me worried.

I had another sleepless night. The following morning I wrote, 'I thought I was out of the woods, but evidently I'm not quite.'

✧

The NST representative duly made the trip to Liverpool from London by train the next day and we met privately in my office at the Cathedral. To my relief, the issue was relatively easily resolved – although to this day my heart goes out to the survivors involved. Precisely because of my nomination to Sheffield, my name had been flagged in connection with a historic safeguarding matter from the 1980s. The case was a deeply distressing one, which ultimately led to an imprisonment for child sexual abuse. It was therefore absolutely right and necessary for the National Safeguarding Team to cross-check some facts, relating to the way I had responded to a disclosure at the time when I was a curate. Some years later, when the case came to court, I had been summoned as a witness. In itself, that was an undeniably uncomfortable experience, but it did mean that I had a kept a record of my actions, so that it was straightforward for me to provide all the information the NST representative required. To my relief, she declared herself satisfied with my responses and reported as much to Sentamu that afternoon. He called me in the evening to confirm that the announcement could now go ahead.

'My goodness,' I noted in my prayer journal, 'I shall certainly arrive thoroughly tempered in the Steel City.'

The next day, Thursday 30th, I received the formal letter of invitation from Downing Street, asking me to confirm my willingness for the Prime Minister to nominate me to the Queen for the See of Sheffield. On account of the urgency, both the invitation and my reply were exchanged by email, with hard copies to follow. I suspect that may have been a first.

On the last day of the month, I wrote in my journal, 'A week from now, all being well, we will be viewing the house together and the news will be out. Meanwhile, I have an appointment in Holy Week to do the examination of my bowel. I feel quite well.'

April 2017

UNEXPECTED TWISTS

The following week was an inevitable blur. Gradually, I had to inform senior colleagues in Liverpool. I also had the opportunity to talk to Peter Burrows, Bishop of Doncaster and to Peter Bradley, Dean of Sheffield. By Tuesday 4th, all the members of the senior team in Sheffield had been informed.

On Wednesday 5th, I made yet another trip down to London – this time for a highly effective media training event. It allowed me to rehearse my draft announcement statement and to undergo a series of mock (but highly realistic) interviews, as if for radio, television and newspaper. It was good to meet up there with the Communications Officer from Sheffield, LJ Buxton. Her professionalism was thoroughly reassuring.

On the morning of Thursday 6th, I had a series of brief appointments in Liverpool, to tell other key Cathedral staff and Diocesan colleagues. The Archbishop's office had alerted both Steven Croft and Philip North and I was moved to receive warm messages of support from each of them. Philip has shown me nothing but encouragement from that moment on. People might understandably wonder if he resented my appointment, but Philip told me that in fact he experienced a profound sense of relief and release at the news of it. His major fear in withdrawing from the process himself was about the chaos and delay it would cause if (as seemed likely to us both) the Diocese had to re-run the CNC process. Thus, the discovery that a re-run was not going to be necessary, and that I was feeling so thoroughly called to the role, was for Philip like nothing less than 'a rescue'.

On Thursday afternoon, Cathy and I drove from Liverpool to Sheffield, via Manchester Airport and the Snake Pass across the Peak District – a route which would become very familiar to us over the following weeks. We checked into a hotel in west Sheffield, desperately hoping not to be recognised. There had recently been a series of occasions when upcoming episcopal appointments had been leaked in advance on social media and I was very keen to avoid that if at all possible. Peter Burrows, and his wife Jane, drove over from Doncaster to eat with us in the evening and to run through the programme for the following day. He was confident that everything was securely in place.

To my relief, there was still no leak first thing the following morning.

At 9.30am, Cathy and I caught a cab from west Sheffield to Manor Top. I had requested that the announcement be made from one of the more deprived neighbourhoods in the Diocese, where the church was fruitfully engaged with the local community, and we had settled on St Swithun's in the Manor Team. I sat nervously in a little vestry off the entrance lobby, watching as the church gradually filled up. Some faces I recognised, most I didn't. The formal announcement was made by 10 Downing Street on the dot of 10am, allowing our press conference to begin.

Following a generous introduction by Bishop Peter, I read out a prepared statement – reproduced at the end of this book on page 113.

I chose to address directly the fact that I was not the preferred candidate of the CNC but the second name, and the line 'Sheffield was never second choice to me' seemed to strike a chord. There were then a series of interviews for regional television and local radio, after which Peter drove me first to Rotherham Minster and then to Doncaster Minster for a repeat of the process. Cathy, meanwhile, was taken for her first sight of Bishopscroft, soon to be our new home.

She and I met up again towards the end of the day for Choral Evensong at the Cathedral, where some of the great and the good of Sheffield had kindly gathered. It was a beautiful spring day and people were evidently full of love and generous affirmation at each of the venues I visited, as well as on social media. By the time we returned to the hotel for a dinner with the senior staff team and their partners, I was full of thanksgiving.

The following morning, I was able to visit Bishopscroft myself for the first time, and to meet members of the household staff. That day truly felt like a new and more spacious era was beginning, especially because, after several highly pressured weeks in which it had been necessary to keep the news of my appointment strictly confidential, everything was out in the open. The sun was still shining, which felt symbolic: for months we had lived under a Sheffield cloud, but now the sky was blue overhead – or so it seemed. In my journal that morning I noted, 'For the first time in ages, I hope now to be able to draw breath.'

It was in a spirit of relief and gratitude that Cathy and I stopped for a pub lunch at The Fox Inn, on the outskirts of Sheffield and the edge of the Peak District, on our way home to Liverpool. If I was looking for symbols, perhaps I should have taken more notice of the football than the weather: in a curious quirk, my beloved Newcastle United were playing Sheffield Wednesday at Hillsborough that very afternoon. Newcastle lost.

The next day was Palm Sunday. This was my eleventh consecutive Holy Week in a cathedral setting. After six in Lichfield, this would be my fifth in Liverpool. I have learned to savour the sacred rhythm of the eight days from Palm Sunday to Easter Day, and to follow the events in the life of Jesus through the week as closely as I can, treating it as a week of 'retreat at home'. I ask my PA to try to avoid scheduling any routine meetings, so that I can prioritise my participation on the unfolding pattern of the worship. This year would prove a bit of an exception to that rule.

Palm Sunday was beautiful, and the congregations at the Cathedral's morning Choral Eucharist and the afternoon Choral Evensong were predictably generous with congratulations and good wishes. On the Monday of Holy Week, the Diocesan Chrism Eucharist was another delight – not only the worship, but the chance to share lunch with so many clergy and lay leaders from across the Diocese of Liverpool in the Cathedral afterwards. Again, Bishop Paul was characteristically thoughtful in inviting the congregation to celebrate my appointment with applause.

On the Tuesday I felt as if everything was progressing nicely. I heard from the Provincial Registrar that dates had been agreed for two of the formal legal steps in the process for my appointment. The election of the new bishop by the Chapter of Sheffield Cathedral would take place in early May, and the Confirmation of Election on 7 June, with a consecration likely to follow on 22nd.

'It's good to be looking back on Friday,' I noted in my journal, 'and forward to the summer.' I wrote about how moving I found it to go through all the email greetings and messages of congratulations.

On the Wednesday I caught an early train to London for a scheduled sigmoidoscopy to resolve the concerns previous tests had raised. It wasn't a procedure I'd ever had before, and I wasn't really very sure what to expect. The hospital staff were compassionate and kind, but there's an irreducible indignity about it. For one thing, I was taken to the theatre dressed only in a cotton gown and paper pants – pants with a great vent in the back. For another, a preliminary enema is required, with repeated dashes to the loo. Only then was I taken down to the theatre.

The consultant was excellent, explaining to me what was involved and why. At first, as he and his colleagues got ready, there was a relaxed atmosphere and some light banter. So I knew at once, just a few seconds after the procedure itself was underway, that he had found a problem. The mood changed instantly, to one of chilly concentration as the consultant reported what he was seeing on his screen, from the camera in my bowel. He took a couple of biopsies, so that a clinical diagnosis would be made, but he made no attempt to hide his impression of what he had found. 'It's bad news,' he said. 'But things will now move quite quickly. You'll need treatment and almost certainly surgery. What we need to do next is to discover how localised the problem is.'

I remember blurting out something to the effect that it had just been announced that I had a new job, and that I was about to move house. The consultant was gentle but firm. 'This must come first,' he said.

I suspect I was in a bit of a trance as I made my way from the clinic to Euston, to catch a train back to Liverpool. As I walked, I phoned Cathy to break the news to her. 'Bad news, I'm afraid,' I said. 'It's cancer.' Over the course of our marriage, Cathy and I have generally tried to laugh at ourselves, not least at times of difficulty or crisis. By this time, I had been shaving my head smooth for 15 years, and so perhaps it was inevitable that I heard myself add, 'At least I won't lose my hair during chemotherapy.' It turns out Cathy had been about to say the very same thing but thought I might not be quite ready for that joke.

On the train home, I inadvertently shared the news with my Liverpool Cathedral PA, Clare. I had composed a message intended for Cathy, lamenting that I might not become Bishop of Sheffield after all, or might be an extremely short-lived one – and by mistake I sent the message to Clare instead. Of course, in the following days it helped very much that she knew, but I hadn't planned to tell her at once, and certainly not in that way.

The following day, back in Liverpool on Maundy Thursday, I noted in my journal, 'Ah, that was not in the script. All is not well, after all. I have cancer in my colon, and I don't yet know what the full implications of that might be. The move to Sheffield must be in doubt again... Everything will depend on whether the cancer is localised or widespread. If it's local, there's every chance we will be looking back on this some years from now. If it's not, I may need to draw up a bucket list. Poor Cathy, what a load to burden her with.'

I had stopped using that Methodist Covenant Prayer at some point in March, when it was clear that I would be nominated for the See of Sheffield after all. In Holy Week, I began to use it again. It was the gift of God that Cathy and I were coming to terms with this development on Maundy Thursday, Good Friday, Holy Saturday and Easter Day – the perfect time to ponder mortality, salvation and the hope of life beyond the grave. Of course we were shaken, and of course there were tears. But both of us were blessed with an intense sense of the presence of God in those days, and of gratitude for the life we had been given, and the love which surrounded us.

I was very unsure who to tell about this latest crisis. For several reasons, my instinct was to keep the circle of those in the know as small as possible. For one thing, I am quite the most introverted person I know. I can perform an extrovert role, but at a cost. My own wellbeing is most enhanced when I have space to myself, and in this situation I knew I would need some privacy. But I was also mindful of the situation in Sheffield. Given all the turmoil the Diocese had already faced, I was wary of introducing fresh uncertainty, at least until I knew the full extent of the challenge I was facing. Thirdly, I happen to know another bishop who, when diagnosed with cancer while in post, chose the opposite path: he put the information in the public domain more or less from the start. I remember him telling me that he might be more careful if he could revisit his decision, because his cancer became the one lens through which people then related to him, as if he had the 'C-word' stamped on his forehead. 'I felt like I had become a temporary bishop,' he said. With this in mind, in the very first few days, Cathy and I told almost no one.

This is something I would do differently if I could go back. To my shame, I didn't stop to consider with any care what Cathy's needs might be in this situation and who she might need to tell.

Of course, I did have to tell Archbishop Sentamu, and when I did so his reaction was robust and reassuring: 'This is the devil,' he told me. 'Hold fast to Jesus. We go on as before.'

I was less certain. In my journal I wrote, 'My best guess is that there is still more cancer to be found. But what that will mean in terms of a prognosis is absolutely not clear. Thank you for the quality of care I am receiving, which might be a lifesaver.'

On Good Friday, I wrote: 'Well, Lord: this is certainly not the path I would have chosen. Whatever the next week brings, it looks like being a pretty severe road ahead. These are going to be tough days.'

Later that day, however, something really rather wonderful happened. Cathy and I attended a service of meditation in the Lady Chapel of the Cathedral in the afternoon, led by the Canon Missioner, Richard White. In a way I don't recall ever having encountered before, Richard homed in on the role of Simon of Cyrene, drafted in to carry the cross of Jesus, when the Lord became too weak to bear his burden for himself.

'What burdens are you carrying,' Richard asked, 'and with whom could you share the load?'

Both Cathy and I heard the Word of the Lord in that question and resolved to bring a wider circle of praying family and friends into the picture – though I'm aware I was still trying to keep the circle narrower than Cathy would have preferred. In my journal I wrote, 'Back to the Methodist Covenant Prayer, I suppose! Lots of opportunity to enter into the pattern of the Lord's saving death and resurrection.'

On Holy Saturday, I told senior lay and clergy colleagues in Liverpool, some on the phone and some face to face; and my Mum and Dad (both then in their eighties) and our two sons also (over the phone). 'That was tough,' I wrote at the time – and I recall that telling parents and children brought fresh tears.

Late in Holy Week I had learned that a follow-up scan had now been scheduled for Thursday 20 April, the following week. That is when we would learn how widespread the problem might be.

On Easter Day I recorded in my journal, 'Golly, this is a different and unexpected angle on our resurrection hope. Sobering (given how precarious life is for all of us all the time) to realise now that I have in fact been assuming I would live into a healthy retirement.'

And, 'I'm fairly certain there is more cancer to be found in the next few days. It's hard not to interpret every ache and pain in terms of the tumour. I wonder how it will all look, one week today?'

That Easter Day, after the major cathedral celebrations of our Lord's resurrection, both morning and afternoon, my dear clergy colleagues in Liverpool met with Cathy and me to anoint me with oil and to pray for us both. That was absolutely typical of both their affection and care for us, and of their devout faith and trust in God. It left us feeling much loved, as well as much prayed for.

It had become usual for us, in the week after Easter (when many clergy schedule a week of annual leave), to visit my parents, who live in Eastbourne. In April 2017, my Dad was 87 and my Mum 82. They had retired to the south coast in the 1990s and were happily settled there, even though no one else in the family was close by. I am one of four siblings, and I live farthest away. These trips are always precious – but for obvious reasons this one felt even more so. Generally on these visits, if we make the journey by train, my Dad comes alone to the local station to pick us up in the car. On this occasion, on Easter Monday, Mum came too – unsurprisingly, there were more tears in the station car park.

Mum and Dad live close to the Downs and over the years Cathy and I have driven up to a car park on the top of the ridge for a jog. The following day, we enjoyed a run together in the breezy sunshine. There's a point along the route where Cathy often stops, while I go on, just a few hundred metres, well within sight. We both felt fit and strong as we ran, but I did wonder, when I got to my turning point and prepared to head back towards Cathy, about keeling over and feigning death, to get a reaction. I thought better of it. Cathy would probably have punched me. But for both of us, the run was an assertion of life.

'If I'm terminally ill,' I noted, 'it will be some time before the disease runs its course. But every day is a bucket list day.' Both Cathy and I were seeking to relish each and every day, and all that each day had to offer.

The scan required what felt like a pretty brutal dietary preparation from 48 hours out: 24 hours of white meat, white bread and so on; 24 hours of fasting, and then in the final 24 hours a medication called 'Picolax', designed to empty the colon.

On the morning of Thursday 20th, the day of the scan, I wrote in my diary, 'Here we go: in another 8 hours or so, we should at least have a clearer idea of what the coming months hold in store. Dietary preparations for the examination this afternoon have not been fun. I've not eaten any solids since 1pm yesterday, nor any tea or coffee since 9pm last night, so I'm hungry and in caffeine deficit. The laxatives have been extremely effective, however.'

I had the MRI scan at 2pm, followed two hours later by a consultation to receive the results. I vividly recall savouring the steak and tartare sauce sandwich I was served immediately after the scan, then sitting in the corridor waiting to be called in by the consultant, wondering in which of two directions our future path would lead. It felt like a 'left or right' moment.

✧

Cathy was with me. When the consultant saw us, he said at once 'That's all clear.' I understood him to mean, 'That's all local. Everywhere else is clear.' But Cathy understood him to mean, 'The result of this scan is beyond doubt…' So she was still sitting nervously waiting for more information, when I was breathing a sigh of relief. Fortunately, I had interpreted the consultant's first words correctly.

The good news was that the scan had confirmed that the cancer was entirely localised, which opened up good prospects for treatment and a likely cure – albeit involving chemoradiotherapy and surgery. The bad news was that the position of the tumour, very low in the colon, made it likely that a colostomy would be required, and potentially a six-week-long recuperation period after the surgery.

I remember thinking this was not the way I would have chosen to be introduced to a new diocese…

In the last week of April, we made a second visit to the house in Sheffield, to discuss redecoration plans, and to get to know some of the staff who were based there a little better. At that point it felt a little like being guests in their house, and therefore a bit awkward not to tell them about my situation. We would do so, a little later down the line. And on that same day, Friday 28th, I heard from the consultant in London that he would like to arrange one more test to determine whether there was any trace of the cancer in the prostate. He assured me that a date would be found as soon as possible.

May 2017

COMPETING DEMANDS

I am blessed to belong to a remarkable cell group, formed in the summer of 1987 by a few students who, having studied together for three years, were leaving Ridley Hall Theological College in Cambridge to begin ordained ministry. Our first ever meeting was in the first week of May 1988, running from Tuesday lunchtime to Thursday lunchtime. May 2017 saw us meeting for the thirtieth year in a row, with only the venue and perhaps one or two members changing over the years.

At first, we met at a retreat centre in Derbyshire, but for the past 20 years we have met in Gloucestershire. At first there were ten of us, but after three decades only seven were still involved – two having left the ordained ministry of the Anglican Church and one no longer feeling the group was right for him. We are all men, which is inevitable given the era in which we began meeting. All of us are married and all have children – and increasingly, grandchildren. We meet for fellowship and prayer together, to support and care for one another and to offer one another a degree of accountability in what can sometimes be a lonely and rather unaccountable ministry.

Three years of residential theological college training together meant we had strong bonds of trust and mutual respect from the start. Thirty years later, those bonds have only strengthened as we have sought to encourage one another through the ups and downs of ordained ministry, but also the ups and downs of life – not least through the challenges of having and parenting our children. It would be fair to say that, year by year, we need each other to different degrees. This year wasn't the first I had arrived in some distress, but it probably was the time I felt most acutely in need of the kindness of the group. Of course, I found it. I was able to share with them the whole story, and to receive their probing and challenging questions, their generous attention and pastoral encouragement, and their fervent prayer. It made a huge difference, but of course Cathy remained at home and had no access to that support.

At cell I am often able to disconnect entirely from other claims on my attention, but it proved impossible that year. I was on the phone several times over those few days to Dr Blair in London to fix up a date for a biopsy on my prostate. This was the last step before a treatment plan could be finalised. It was necessary to double-check that the cancer was not in my prostate as well as my bowel before dates for chemotherapy and radiotherapy could be fixed. That uncertainty introduced others: it was impossible for me to agree the date for a Service of Consecration, or even for a house move, until the picture was clearer. Indeed, at this point it was not even clear whether treatment would take place in London, in Liverpool or in Sheffield. The Harley Street specialists I had been seeing were keen for me to have my treatment privately in London, and I believe the Church Commissioners would probably have agreed to fund this. My own preference was to have the treatment locally, either in Liverpool or in Sheffield; if I could choose, I knew I would rather have it in Sheffield, after a move. This was mostly psychological: I thought I would cope more easily with the house move followed by treatment, than the reverse. But I was weighing up other considerations too. After five years of living in Liverpool, the chances of my being recognised while attending medical appointments there was surely higher than it would be in Sheffield, where I was still a complete stranger. However, support structures in Liverpool would surely be more developed than in Sheffield. Again, without really being conscious that this is what I was doing, in my balancing of needs I was prioritising my own over Cathy's.

The most vulnerable such date was the one fixed for my ordination as a bishop. Back in April it had been agreed that this would take place on 22 June, and at this point I was proceeding as if that was a firm commitment, while knowing that there were still circumstances which would prevent it from going ahead. So it was that on Thursday 4 May, I travelled from the cell meeting to York via Liverpool (to pick up Cathy and my PA, Clare), for a first meeting with the Canon Precentor at York Minster, to discuss arrangements for the service. It became clear that I would enjoy a certain amount of discretion regarding the content of the service – about the preacher, for example, and some musical choices. I did not dare mention in our conversation the fact that if the imminent biopsy on my prostate indicated a need to proceed urgently with cancer surgery or chemoradiotherapy, I might not be available for a service on that date after all.

Other dates, however, were unaffected by these uncertainties. On Friday 5 May, the College of Canons met at Sheffield Cathedral, as mandated by the Queen, to elect me as their new bishop in accordance with her request. This ancient practice, going back at least to the time of the Reformation, is a legal requirement but unarguably also an anachronism. First, Buckingham Palace has to issue a writ to the Dean of the Cathedral of the Diocese in which the Bishop is to be appointed, requiring the Dean to summon the honorary canons of the Cathedral on a specific date. That document is called a Congé d'Élire (Permission to Elect). In effect, the College of Canons is required to meet in order to give its support to the person nominated by the Crown to be the new bishop. It sounds like a process of which Stalin himself would be proud: an election with only one name on the ballot paper! Then the Dean is required to write to the Canons concerned, summoning them to the Cathedral to conduct the election, warning members of the

College of Canons that they risk being considered 'contumacious' by the Crown if they either fail to attend the election or fail to give their support to the Crown's nominated individual. Despite the mere formality (I don't believe there has ever been an occasion in living memory when someone has been nominated but not elected), I still found it a great encouragement and reassurance to receive a text from the Dean that evening, confirming that the process had been completed, and including a photograph of the signed deed which announced my election as Bishop of Sheffield.

That same day, Friday 5 May, it was announced that Peter Eagles had been appointed Bishop of Sodor and Man and would also be consecrated at the same service on 22 June. Of course, that introduced a double complication. Now it was necessary to share the planning of the discretionary elements of the service with Peter (a delightfully easy experience, as it happens). But I had to do this without telling him about my situation. I was not quite ready to do that yet.

Revisiting my daily prayer journal, I see that on Monday 8 May I noted a new number in the heading for the first time.

I have kept a journal almost daily for nearly 40 years. For each entry I note the date, the time, and the place where I am writing. But on this day, I added another number: 20,299. Monday 8 May was the 20,299th day of my life. Almost every day since then, I have noted the equivalent number. Today (as I write this memoir) is the 22,802nd day of my life.

This has become a spiritual discipline for me. I don't know how long I will live, but I do know that my earthly life is limited: one day I shall die. On that day, there will be a death date to go with my birth date and in between will be the number of my days. I don't know how big that number will be. Back when I began the habit I had not lived

21,000 days. Now I have lived almost 23,000. But however big the number might grow to be, it is nevertheless a limited number. In Psalm 90.12 the psalmist prays, 'So teach us to count our days, that we may gain a wise heart.' I began this practice on that day and have continued ever since.

In other words, one of the early benefits of my illness was to make me freshly aware of my mortality and to help me see more clearly the value of each day. It has motivated me to be much more deliberate to note each passing day, and to seek to make the most of it. As a daily discipline, I seek to give thanks to God for each new day at the start of the day, as I note it in my journal, and then again at the end of the day, for all the blessings it has brought. The uncertainty I was experiencing at that time sharpened my awareness of the limit to how much longer I might live.

'I am seeking to live one day at a time,' I wrote.

On Wednesday 10 May I travelled down to London for yet another medical appointment – this time for a briefing consultation about the biopsy that was scheduled for the following week, and the possible implications for a treatment plan. I came away from that meeting with a huge sense of relief: for the first time, I was given some clarity about the extent of the likely treatment. Probably I would need five to seven weeks of daily radiotherapy sessions (Monday to Friday), each session quite brief. What's more, the consultant had agreed that, almost whatever the outcome of the prostate biopsy, the start of treatment could now wait until late June, after a house move to Sheffield and after the consecration. Even though we hadn't resolved where any treatment would take place, I felt like a great burden of anxiety had been lifted. I could now focus on a good leaving of Liverpool.

Unfortunately, that sense of relief lasted only 24 hours. I had a phonecall from the consultant the very next day, Friday 12th, to say that an interdisciplinary meeting had been held about my case, at which it had been decided that the treatment might need to begin sooner rather than later after all – especially if it proved that the cancer had indeed spread to my prostate.

On Saturday 13 May, I noted for the first time how difficult I was finding it to cope with the experience of being 'yanked' this way and that, by the demands of both the illness and my vocation. One moment I might be taking a phonecall (as I did at about this time), from William Nye, the General Secretary of the Church of England, asking me if I would be willing to chair the Biblical Studies Working Group as part of the Living in Love and Faith (LLF) process. (I said yes, very much feeling thrown in at the deep end.) The next moment, I might be taking a phonecall from the consultant confirming the date, time and place of the biopsy and informing me that the procedure would require a general anaesthetic. I might be receiving an encouraging medical update, followed swiftly by a more worrying one. On that date I also noted in my journal that Cathy and I had named the tumour 'Lucille', after the Country and Western ballad, 'You picked a fine time to leave me, Lucille'. It helped us to domesticate the tumour and its potentially sinister implications.

On Friday 18th, I was back on a train to London, this time with Cathy to accompany me at least as far as Euston, if not to the clinic itself. We had to set off very early from Liverpool Lime Street in order for me to check in to the clinic at 7.30am. Once there, I was treated with great courtesy and kindness by those I encountered: from the porter who showed me to the preparation room and took me to the theatre, to the nurses, the anaesthetist and the consultant. It was the first time in my life I had been under a general anaesthetic, but I was carefully briefed. I was warned to expect a cold sensation in my arm and a funny taste in my mouth. I remember recognising those; but the next thing I knew, I was coming round in the recovery room, a little light-headed, but with no residual pain at all. I was able to text Cathy to let her know all was well, and after I had been kept under observation for a short time, and had demonstrated that I could pass urine, I was discharged. Cathy had begun to walk towards the theatre as I walked towards the station and we met up for a coffee halfway. Amazingly, we were back in Liverpool by 2.30pm.

It was an anxious week of waiting for the results to come through, but I had a nice distraction on Wednesday 24th, when my episcopal robes arrived from J&M Sewing Services in Newcastle upon Tyne: a new purple cassock, and the 'rochet and chimere' in which I would, God willing, be consecrated in due course. I had first used J&M as an ordinand, when I ordered my first ever set of clerical robes, in which I was ordained deacon in 1987 and priest in 1988. Astonishingly, they still had my measurements on record, so I asked them to use those for the new robes. Most of the kit fitted perfectly: I am still the same height as I was 30 years ago, and the robes themselves are roomy and forgiving enough to accommodate the extent to which my body shape has changed over the years. But I did have to send back the cincture (a liturgical cummerbund), as it was several inches too small and could not pass even as a tight fit. Funnily enough, I had recently started to worry about some discernible weight loss – so it was good to be reminded that there was plenty of spare weight to lose!

Thursday 25 May was Ascension Day – another great day in a cathedral calendar. In 2017 it was unfortunately overshadowed for me by our need to clear the house. Cathy and I were sorting through our belongings, in an attempt to lighten the ship, when a phonecall came. It was the London consultant with good news: my prostate was clear of cancer. No fewer than 30 samples had been taken, from every part of the organ, and all were fine. That was a great relief and significantly simplified the treatment plan.

On Monday 29 May, I entered my final full working week as Dean of Liverpool. I would miss the stellar colleagues with whom it was my privilege to serve there, the extraordinary Cathedral building, and the adventure and risk-taking it invited; but also the city and people of Liverpool, in all their sunny good humour and warmth.

That week I also received confirmation that the treatment would now be scheduled not in Liverpool or in London but in Sheffield, after our house move. Given the symptoms I was starting to experience – which involved an upset stomach requiring frequent dashes to the toilet, repeated doses of immodium, and noticeably increased backache – this was the scenario I would have chosen. Again, the confirmation of it came as a great relief. I was also, however, impatient to get started with the treatment.

June 2017

ALL CHANGE

On 14 June we moved from The Deanery, 1 Cathedral Close in Liverpool, to Bishopscroft, the official residence of the Bishops of Sheffield. This was courtesy of the Britannia removals company, who did a great job – although it might have been fun to employ their wonderfully named competitor, 'Bishops Move'.

Either side of that removal came two significant liturgical occasions, both at York Minster: the ceremony for the Confirmation of Election, and the Service of Consecration. Before it there were two other great acts of worship in Liverpool Cathedral: Pentecost Sunday, when we celebrated (in fine style) the outpouring of the Holy Spirit upon the Church of Jesus Christ, and Trinity Sunday, when we not only celebrated the culmination of the Christian liturgical year and the revelation of God, Father, Son and Holy Spirit, but also said our farewell.

The first of the two services at York Minster was the Confirmation of Election on Monday 5 June in the evening. Someone has described this service as 'Choral Evensong meets Gilbert and Sullivan'. The occasion combines all the solemnity and choral beauty of Evensong with something of a pantomine. The Confirmation of Election itself is a legal step, dating back to medieval times, in which the credentials of the person elected to be bishop are examined. It's the ancient equivalent of producing photo ID to prove that you are who you say you are, and a Disclosure and Barring Service (DBS) certificate to prove that you are a person of good repute and in good standing. The process is a choreographed dialogue, mostly between two legal representatives: one acting on behalf of the Archbishop, whose role is to require various assurances, and another acting on behalf of the 'would-be' bishop, whose role is to provide them. These days the process is never in doubt, but I was still delighted to have HHJ Clement Goldstone KC acting on my behalf. Clem was then the Recorder of Liverpool and, with his wife Vanessa, had become good friends to Cathy and me during our time in the city. He is an eminent member of the Jewish community in Manchester. He had graciously once invited us to his home to share a family Shabbat meal. Given the dark history of anti-semitism in the Christian church, not least in York, I was especially grateful to Clem for agreeing to act on my behalf in this arcane and mightily peculiar Christian ceremony. In fact, I recall a good-humoured exchange between Clem and Archbishop Sentamu, in the aisle before the service began, in which that history (and the at least modestly redemptive nature of this arrangement) was acknowledged.

During the service, which was attended by the senior staff teams in both Liverpool and Sheffield, Archbishop Sentamu preached on Joshua 1. That was, in fact, the appointed Old Testament reading for the day – but in exhorting me to 'be strong and very courageous', Sentamu managed to reference my illness without actually naming it.

By the end of that service, I was legally the Bishop of Sheffield, and no longer Dean of Liverpool. Happy as I was to enter into the new calling for which I felt God had carefully prepared me, I can't deny that I also felt a great deal of loss. My term as Dean of Liverpool had been the most fruitful, the most fulfilling and, frankly, the most fun of my ordained ministry. It is customary for a Cathedral Chapter to present a gift to a departing Dean, and in the circumstances – given how formative my five years in Liverpool had been for my leadership – I knew exactly what I most wanted. Part of the uniform of a bishop is an episcopal ring, worn on the third finger of the right hand. Invited by the chapter to stipulate a farewell gift, I chose a ring. It is a simple silver signet ring, bearing the logo of Liverpool Cathedral (a double-arm cross, which echoes the 'footprint' of the Cathedral). It arrived that week, more than meeting my hopes for it.

Thursday 8 June that year was a general election. It was a wet and windy day. Ultimately, it led to a minority government, led by the Conservative Party, but requiring the support of the Democratic Unionist Party of Northern Ireland. That was the day boxes arrived from the removal company, to enable me to clear the Dean's Office of books. Meanwhile, Cathy and I were making repeated trips to the local recycling and waste site. The political landscape seemed to mirror our own personal uncertainty about what the future would hold.

Our farewell from Liverpool took place at the Choral Eucharist for Trinity Sunday, 11 June. At my installation as Dean, in September 2012, the central symbolic act was the moment when I was clothed by Chapter colleagues in my Liverpool Cathedral cope. It was a fitting symbolic gesture, then, when I was 'divested' of the cope at the end of this service, and handed in my keys and electronic passes. That day I had preached on 'the Grace' with which St Paul concludes his second letter to the Corinthians (2 Corinthians 13.13). I had presided at Holy Communion for the last time. I remember that I burst into tears during the final hymn, after which the usual speeches and presentations followed. By the time Cathy and I got home, we were emotionally exhausted, but also enriched by the kindness and enormous generosity of the congregation at the Cathedral, and of the wider Liverpool community.

We moved house a few days later, on Wednesday 14th. It is well known that clergy are a removal company's nightmare: we generally have a ridiculous quantity of books to pack up. But in our case, we also have a ridiculous quantity of glassware and bric-a-brac, and the speedy efficiency and uncomplaining patience of the removal company was impressive. I have an absurd collection of Bible commentaries, which inflates the number of books; Cathy has an abusrd collection of bric-a-bac, incuding glassware and pottery. The vans were on their way by noon. Cathy and I followed in separate cars in the mid-afternoon, waved off the Cathedral Close by friends and neighbours.

Built in 1914, Bishopscroft is a beautiful Arts and Crafts property set in spacious gardens, located in West Sheffield. We spent our first night there in what we call 'the Church Commissioners' bedroom': a bedroom reserved for official guests and furnished by the Church Commissioners, who own the house. We were still feeling very much like guests in our new house at that point! I am blessed with a considerable capacity for focus, and my focus over the next few days was to clear the house of boxes and to make the place as much a home as possible, as quickly as possible. I noted on Saturday 17 June that I had covered four miles, without once setting foot outside the house!

Bishopscroft is the ninth home Cathy and I have made together in (what was then) almost 30 years of married life. We have, necessarily, become quite skilled at the process of inhabiting a new place. For me, taking occupation requires the unpacking of boxes. In particular, I need to get my collection of Bible commentaries onto shelves in my study. Once that is accomplished, I can begin to settle. In my journal for Friday 16 June, I noted, 'My commentaries are up on the shelves and looking good.'

✧

On the following day, Sunday 18 June, Cathy surprised me by picking a beautiful arrangement of flowers from the garden and placing them in a vase on the Holy Table in the Bishopscroft chapel. It's something I would never have thought of doing, but it felt like another highly symbolic moment – beautifying the place of worship in the house as a mark of its priority for us.

Our recently engaged son and future daughter-in-law, living and working as missionaries in Japan, arrived back in England on Tuesday 20th and we collected them from the airport in Manchester. To our great relief, they quickly fell in love with the house and garden at Bishopscroft and decided that was where their UK-based wedding blessing would take place. This was just as well, as by then I had cancelled the booking on the Lady Chapel at Liverpool Cathedral!

One of the stresses of this period was that no firm treatment plan had yet been finalised. This journal entry of 21 June is typical of that time, 'I wish I could get progress on a treatment plan. It does seem to be taking for ever.' By then it was almost nine weeks since the tumour had been discovered, and a month since the biopsy results on my prostate were known. As it happens, the plan would be firmed up the very next day – which just happened to be the date of the Service of Consecration at York Minster.

I travelled up to York for a rehearsal of the service on the afternoon of the 21st, and later met up with members of my family for dinner and Compline (Night Prayer) at Bishopsthorpe. It was the first time I'd been there since the interview seven months before and the oddity of the situation was very real to me. Also present were Peter Eagles and Gail and their son. I was due to be consecrated as a bishop alongside Peter the following day.

The following day began with Morning Prayer in the Chapel at Bishopsthorpe. I remember Archbishop Sentamu telling Peter Eagles and me that he hoped our consecration as bishops would mean that we would spend more time with Jesus and not less. I have called that implied exhortation to mind more than once since then. After breakfast, we made our way to York Minster for the service at 11am. Cathy caught the hem of her wide-legged jumpsuit on the door and momentarily lost her balance as she exited our car in the Minster car park. She might easily have landed nose-first on the tarmac, but recovered with the elegance you would expect of a Judo black belt.

My memories of the service itself are sketchy. I remember that a verger kindly found me an iron so that I could smooth out my rumpled 'rochet' (a white cotton vestment). Also that some preliminary declaration and oaths of allegiance were made in the Lady Chapel just before the service began – to the Christian faith as the Church of England has received it, to the Archbishop of York as Primate of the Northern Province (in which the Diocese of Sheffield sits) and to the monarch. I remember the sense of collegiality and kinship I formed with Peter Eagles, whom I had previously never met, as we prepared to go through this experience of ordination together. I remember the wonderful array of smiling faces, representing every stage of my ordained ministry, and even a number of school and university friends who had known me before I was ever ordained, but also lots of people from Sheffield, there to welcome me to our new Diocese. The experience reminded me a little of my wedding day: to be the focus of such an outpouring of love and rejoicing, of prayer and goodwill, was deeply moving.

Our oldest son Jonathan read the Old Testament reading, and did so word-perfectly – and then concluded with a definite cough as he uttered the required phrase 'This is the Word of the Lord,' to indicate his scepticism. The reading had been taken from the Book of Wisdom which is from the Apocrypha – so not definitively a part of the Christian Scriptural canon as the Church of England has received it.

An extraordinary sermon was preached by the remarkable Revd Professor David Wilkinson. David is a long-term friend of mine and it was my suggestion that he should be invited to deliver the sermon. But he demonstrated his characteristic generosity by researching and referencing Peter Eagles' ministry, gifts and passions as fully as he did mine. I remember that Archbishop Sentamu allowed moments of simple silence during the liturgy. I remember that my father David, himself a bishop, was able to join in the laying on of hands at the moment of my consecration; and I remember the long hug I was able to share with Philip North during the Peace.

Perhaps inevitably, at the end of the service I found myself caught at the Great West Door of the Minster as people filed out, talking with those who had so kindly attended. As a result, I didn't get to the nearby reception until almost 2pm, an hour or so after the service had ended.

It was somehow predictable that this was the moment I would finally get my referral to the Sheffield Teaching Hospitals NHS Trust. In fact, I had felt the notification of a new voicemail buzz on the mobile phone in my cassock pocket during the service, but of course it was only as I walked from the Minster to the reception that I was able to listen to it. It confirmed that the medical handover from London to Sheffield was now complete and gave me a number to call to arrange a consultation to agree a treatment plan.

By late afternoon we were driving back to Sheffield in a state of thankful exhaustion. I was glad to finally escape the crowds and to reflect on a wonderful day. Legally, I had held the office of Bishop of Sheffield since the Confirmation of Election on the 9th, and was now ordained as a bishop and able to perform the liturgical functions of a bishop. However, I would not begin to exercise my public ministry until one final step had been completed.

Every new diocesan bishop must also formally be installed in the Cathedral Church. That service was not due to take place until 23 September. This allowed a very timely two-month period of 'downtime' in which the treatment could be accommodated. I would also begin some initial induction meetings with key stakeholders in the Diocese and in South Yorkshire and the East Riding, and some literal exploration of the Diocese. I had never lived in the region before, and the geography was entirely new to me, so the summer weeks also provided me with a welcome opportunity to do some touring of deaneries, under the radar.

The day after the Service of Consecration I had a further communication with a consultant at Weston Park Cancer Hospital in Sheffield – amazingly, just a five-minute drive from our new house. 'The best development of the day,' I noted in my journal, 'was a set of phonecalls with a consultant here in Sheffield. Finally it looks as if a treatment plan can begin. I go to see him next Wednesday, and should then get a first scoping scan the next week and begin radiotherapy about five weeks after that. He seems very good.'

The appointment on Wednesday 28th also happened to be the thirtieth anniversary of my ordination as a deacon in Durham Cathedral in 1987. My appointment with the consultant that day was undoubtedly helpful, but gave me a rather bleaker assessment both of the demands of the five weeks of chemotherapy and radiotherapy which were being proposed, and of the implications should there be a recurrence of the cancer down the road. The consultant said that would be 'tricky'. When I asked what he meant by 'tricky' he replied, 'Well, it's usually fatal.'

It was also on that visit that I was given three tiny tattoos across my abdomen – each one no bigger than a pinhead – to provide the radiotherapy technicians with a triangulated target. The tattoos are permanent: I can find them to this day. Every now and again in social situations the question is asked, 'Do you have a tattoo?' I used to be able to answer 'No,' not because I disapprove of tattoos (in fact, I might easily have had a small and discreet one done at some stage), but because I never got around to having one.

These days, I'm not quite sure what a truthful answer would be.

July 2017

ENDURING TREATMENT

On the first day of July I took a very welcome phonecall from Weston Park Hospital to say that my treatment had been brought forward a week. It would begin on Thursday 6th – just two weeks after my consecration as a bishop. This came as a great relief to me. The backache and frequent visits to the toilet had now persisted for weeks, and I found myself regarding the treatment as a sort of 'striking back'. I knew the process was likely to prove gruelling, but I had decided to focus on how gruelling it must be for 'Lucille'.

The regime involved taking large, pink chemo tablets at 8.30 each day, morning and evening, Monday to Friday, and attending an appointment for additional radiotherapy. This regime ran across six weeks: two days in week one, then four weeks of five days, finishing with three days in the sixth week. In week four, after fifteen days, the chemotherapy tablet dose increased, adding to the cumulative challenge. It was only in retrospect that I appreciated the value of beginning with only a part week. The radiotherapy was generally swift and straightforward – often I was in and out in just 20 minutes. It involved checking in for the procedure and waiting to be called, before stripping off and lying on a trolley-bed with no more than a paper napkin to cover my modesty. Skilled technicians would target the equipment, guided by my new tattoos, and for a few minutes each day the tumour would be 'zapped'. My only responsibility was to lie still. On most occasions, I did not find that difficult to achieve. But on one of the days, a draught blew the napkin off my body and onto the floor. Lying there naked as the day I was born, it was really very hard not to get up to retrieve a covering.

My radiotherapy appointments were a blunderbuss shot at my diary. The five appointments each week, Monday to Friday, might be at any time of the day, from early morning to late evening. Most of these were mid-afternoon, though some were early in the day and others late in the evening, apparently randomly. Yet, by the grace of God, not one required me to shift other commitments which had been entered into the diary.

When my diary was full in the morning, the radiotherapy was invariably scheduled for the afternoon, and vice versa. On the day I was required to travel into London to pay homage to the Sovereign (as all newly appointed diocesan bishops are required to do), the radiotherapy slot was one of only two occasions when it was scheduled in the evening. It felt like a small gift of God's providence.

I was also a little anxious that, during the course of my 25 visits to the hospital I might be recognised by another patient or a member of staff, prompting inevitable questions about my health. But as far as I know, that didn't happen – and if it did, those who recognised me were perfectly discreet. That too felt like a gift.

One particular appointment sticks in my mind, not for any reason to do with the treatment. Usually I could find a parking space by the roadside, very close to the hospital. On this occasion, there was none. I then had to do an about turn in my car and drive back the way I had come to a pay and display car park in a nearby shopping precinct. It was camera-controlled, and drivers were required to enter their car number-plate into the ticket machine. I was in a bit of a hurry to ensure that I made the appointment in time, but thought I had done everything necessary. So I was a bit surprised and annoyed a week or so later to receive a fine through the post. Evidenced by a photograph of my car, it demonstrated that the ticket in the windscreen did not match the number-plate of the car. I had mistakenly entered the number for our own car, when I was driving the episcopal one. I have never appealed a fine with such confidence that it would be repealed: I had a valid ticket, for a car registered to me with the DVLA matching the number I had entered, and the car I had parked was also registered to me. It was a simple mistake. There was no question whether or not I had actually paid to park there. I provided photographic evidence of my own, and also a reference to the fact that I had been attending an appointment at the local hospital for cancer treatment. But my appeal was rejected. In my frustration, I wrote to the ombudsman to complain: the reply was carefully and kindly written, but expressed regret that the contractor was within their rights to levy the penalty. I am still cross about it to this day!

It's an idle gesture, I realise, but I have also resolved never to use that car park again.

The treatment dominated July and became cumulatively challenging. The weekends became increasingly precious as respite. Each Wednesday, after every five sessions of radiotherapy, my appointment was followed by an assessment conversation with the doctor in charge of the treatment, mostly just to check that I was tolerating the regime adequately.

My journal indicates that I pretty much sailed through the first week, which included a trip to York on Monday 10th, to join the other bishops who were leading work streams on the Living in Love and Faith (LLF) programme. They were gathered for a meeting of the General Synod, which I had decided not to engage with until after my Installation. But it was clear that LLF was going to be a major commitment in the first few years of my tenure as Bishop of Sheffield, so I felt it was right to join in with that from the start. It is an indication of the lack of clarity about the process at its inception that, after that first meeting, I noted in my journal, 'No one is quite sure, I think, what we are being asked to do or how we will go about it.'

That first week also included a trip to London to meet up with the journalist David Conn. I knew David's name because he has written widely on football, and I'm a mildly obsessive fan. Some years before, I had read his book The Beautiful Game? and in October 2016 I saw a piece on 'the burning injustice of Orgreave' he had published in The Guardian. After I was appointed, I contacted him to request a meeting. The so-called Battle of Orgreave took place in June 1984 during the year-long nationwide miners' strike. In South Yorkshire, it is widely believed that the police used excessive force that day and for forty years now, ex-miners and other campaigners have been calling for a public inquiry. I share the view that an inquiry is necessary (and in time inevitable), and since Orgreave lies in the Diocese of Sheffield I felt a pastoral responsibility to help those whose lives were most seriously affected to find closure, and to ensure every possible lesson is learned for the future.

Over the past six years, I have gladly continued to meet with representatives of the Orgreave Truth and Justice Campaign and I share their view that only a full inquiry has any chance of delivering truth and justice. David Conn is a highly regarded, award-winning investigative journalist and he has been pressing for an inquiry for many years. It was good of him to meet with me, and I found his help extremely useful. Sadly, those of us who have been calling for an inquiry have been unsuccessful so far. It is more than possible that a new government will change that.

Towards the end of week two of the treatment, I made another trip to London – this time for the peculiar but utterly wonderful experience of paying homage to the Queen. The reigning monarch is head of the

Church of England, and every new diocesan bishop is required to pledge allegiance to the Sovereign in that capacity. Pandemic exceptions aside, this takes place in what amounts to a private audience. In my case, it happened on Tuesday 18 July – and once again I had Peter Eagles, the new Bishop of Sodor and Man, for company. We were required to report to Buckingham Palace at 11.30am for a ceremony which took place at noon.

Once admitted to the palace, I was shown to a robing room, where Peter was waiting, along with James Newcome (then Bishop of Carlisle and the Clerk of the Closet, who presents bishops to the Sovereign on these occasions) and the Sub-Dean of the Chapel Royal (Deputy Clerk of the Closet). They would also be our companions for lunch after the ceremony. Once we had robed, we were escorted through the corridors of the palace to a lobby outside the room where the homage would take place. There we were introduced to the Queen's Equerry and to the Lord Chancellor, who would facilitate the ritual. In 2017, the Lord Chancellor was David Lidington MP.

When the moment came, I was ushered inside the state room to find the Queen waiting for me at the far end. The equerry presented me at the door and I crossed the room to shake her Majesty by the hand and to greet her. The Queen then took her seat and I was invited to kneel before her at a prayer-desk with my hands clasped in front of me. The Queen then put her hands around mine and I was asked to repeat the words of an ancient oath, as they were spoken for me by the Lord Chancellor:

'I Peter Jonathan, having been elected, confirmed and consecrated Bishop of Sheffield do hereby declare that Your Majesty is the only supreme governor of this your realm in spiritual and ecclesiastical things as well as in temporal and that no foreign prelate or potentate has any jurisdiction within this realm and I acknowledge that I hold the said bishopric as well the spiritualities as the temporalities thereof only of Your Majesty and for the same temporalities I do my homage presently to Your Majesty so help me God. God save Queen Elizabeth.'

As far as I recall, I managed to get the words out reasonably intelligibly!

The Queen then then stood up and gently helped me to my feet and at once took responsibility for the conversation, so that I wasn't left wondering whether or not it was my place to say something. First Her Majesty asked how I had found the transition from Liverpool to Sheffield. Then she told me that though most people might suppose Sheffield to be an urban diocese, she knew it to be more than the city, and that it has considerable rural parts. No doubt the Queen had been briefed ahead of this moment – but she was then ninety-three years old, and I was astonished how full of energy and grace I found her.

If the average tenure of a diocesan bishop in the Church of England is 10 years, and there are (say) 40 dioceses, then the Queen must have performed this ceremony about 4 times a year. By the time I paid homage, Elizabeth II had been Queen for 65 years – she must have been through this process more than 250 times. But I would not have known it: there was nothing jaded or perfunctory about her presence. And immediately afterwards, she had to repeat the ceremony for Peter Eagles. Like me, he found Her Majesty to be fully present and remarkably sharp.

Towards the end of the ritual, a Bible is held out to the new Bishop, who is expected to kiss it. As one who loves the scriptures, this presented no difficulties to me. Each new Bishop has the opportunity of choosing the page at which the Bible will be open. I had opted for 2 Corinthians 8.9 – a text which concludes the passage on which I would be preaching at the Service of Installation in September: 'For you know the generous act of our Lord Jesus Christ, that though he was rich, yet for your sakes he became poor, so that by his poverty you might become rich.' I felt called to make generosity a key theme of my early ministry in Sheffield and this verse seemed to me to be an excellent foundation for it.

At the end of my audience with the Queen, as we walked to the exit door, I was braced for her to ask why I had chosen this text. I had been primed that this was a question she liked to ask; but it never came. Apparently, she later told Bishop James, her Clerk of the Closet, that she was kicking herself for having forgotten!

After the homage we were served a very hospitable lunch, but I was still able to catch the 3pm train from St Pancras, which got me back to Sheffield in time for a radiotherapy appointment at 5.40pm.

Meanwhile, more routinely, and starting in week three of the treatment, I was attempting to visit each of the twelve deaneries of the Diocese for at least half a day each. This was simply a way of getting my bearings geographically, and as a pilgrimage of prayer. I wasn't setting up meetings with clergy or lay leaders at this point, beyond a series of one-to-one appointments with the senior staff team and area deans at Bishopscroft. Instead, when I was out and about in the deaneries, my PA was choosing some rather random landmarks for me to find, across a deanery at a time, rather like a treasure hunt. I got to four deaneries during week three: Snaith and Hatfield, Doncaster, Hallam and Ecclesall. The former were among those furthest from our house; the latter the two nearest.

On the last day of week three, Cathy and I drove down to Oxford for a delightful meal and a helpful meeting with Bishop Steven Croft, the previous Bishop of Sheffield, and his wife Ann. It was especially useful to hear where Steven thought the key assets in the Diocese were to be found, the key areas of strength and weakness, and the areas of unfinished business he had left behind. I came away encouraged by his perspectives.

But that third week of treatment was also the point at which the cumulative effects became more challenging. On Sunday 23rd, I noted in my journal, 'Gosh this is hard work, O God.' But on Monday 24th, I passed the halfway point of the 25 sessions of radiotherapy: I had undergone 13 and had only 12 left to complete.

Until this point, I had still managed at least a short jog two or three times a week. That stopped on Sunday 30 July, in the middle of week four: I no longer had the energy to do it. I noted in my journal that I was feeling 'pretty grotty'. By evening during the week, and at weekends, I was increasingly inclined to lie on the sofa, under a blanket, watching whatever sport happened to be on TV. The cumulative impact of the treatment was undoubtedly exacerbated by the required increase in chemotherapy tablets in the final two weeks.

August 2017

WELCOME RECUPERATION

Thursday 3 August marked the beginning of my fifth and final week of treatment.

That day, I wrote in my journal, 'The cumulative impact of the treatment is mounting. I'm v glad of empty evenings: by about 8pm I'm done in. There's a band of red tenderness developing around my midriff.'

And on the Saturday, 'Golly, that was a tough day yesterday. I spent most of it lying on the sofa. It's the evenings which are hardest, when I take the second chemo tablet on top of the radiotherapy.'

With a little careful management of my energy, I was able to maintain my round of deanery visits. I went to Tankersley and Ecclesfield on the 3rd, Attercliffe and Laughton on the 8th, Rotherham and Wath on the 12th and West Doncaster and Adwick le Street on the 15th (the final two visits coming – blessedly – after the treatment finished). Some days I did manage an appointment or two, with civic leaders, key clergy and lay people in the Diocese. But towards the end of the process my capacity was very limited.

On Wednesday 9th I paid my final visit to the radiotherapy unit at Weston Park. In many hospitals, it is customary for a patient to 'clang' a bell to mark the end of a course of treatment. It's a nicely defiant gesture. I would quite like to have done it, but was wary of doing anything which might draw additional attention to my presence there. I gave the bell an inner salute as I passed it on my way out.

On Thursday 10th it was a great relief not to have to make my way down to the hospital, but even more so not to have to take the chemo tablets. By the end I had developed quite an aversion to them. The following day, Cathy and I celebrated our 33rd wedding anniversary.

It's a measure of how uncertain I was still feeling about the cancer that I wrote in my journal 'I wonder how many more I shall be able to enjoy? My times are in your hands, O God.'

However, quite quickly after the final session of treatment, I began to feel better, almost by the day. Within a week, on Thursday 17th, I noted, 'This is more like it. I've woken feeling as well as I have felt for some weeks.' And two days later: 'I've woken feeling fit and well after a good night's sleep. I am recovering now, I can tell.' And on Monday 21st: 'Yesterday was my first day without any tablets for weeks. No chemo, no immodium, no ibuprofen, no paracetamol, no cocodamol.'

The sense of respite was doubtless amplified by the imminent prospect of our son Tom's marriage to Rosa. Their wedding was due to take place in Rosa's hometown of Santa Fe, New Mexico, on 1 September, and Cathy and I were planning to go out a week or so beforehand, to make a bit of a holiday of the trip. Foolishly, I hadn't anticipated that my cancer treatment would be a concern to travel insurers, but of course, it was. The cheapest quote I could get for cover was an eye-watering £600!

On Monday 14th, a couple of dates came through from the hospital. I was due to have MRI and CT scans on 28 September, to assess the effectiveness of the initial stage of the treatment. That would be followed by a meeting with the consultant on 5 October to receive the results. The first of those dates presented a logistical challenge: it would fall in the week between the service at Sheffield Cathedral at which I was to be installed on 23 September, and the Service of Wedding Blessing at Bishopscroft for Tom and Rosa on 30 September (arranged for friends and family unable to make the trip to the United States).

Given the daunting six-week interlude between the end of the treatment and the follow-up scans, it was wonderful to have a trip abroad. Cathy and I flew from Manchester to Denver, Colorado on 23 August for a week of holiday. We spent the first few days in the Rockies, and then returned to Denver to pick up our oldest son, Jon, before making a road trip of the journey to Santa Fe. I did occasionally discover the limits to my recovery: climbing back up the Rio Grande after descending into the canyon, for example. But for much of the time I was feeling fit and strong enough to enjoy the sights – including some white-water rafting and a visit to some hot springs. Jon had his own good news to rejoice in: he and Izzy were expecting their first baby and earlier in the month their 20-week scan had shown that their baby girl was growing perfectly normally. The whole week of holiday felt like a feast of life.

We arrived safely in Santa Fe on Tuesday 29th, and met up with Rosa's parents for the first time, over a restaurant meal. Both John and Teresa come from large and long-established Santa Fe families. In fact, both are the youngest of seven children, and they have also had seven children. The Griego clan is huge, and we spent much of the next two days meeting its members and enjoying lavish Latin American hospitality.

On the last day of the month, there was a wedding rehearsal. It was only then that I discovered that the wedding would be an outdoor ceremony in the church grounds. When I asked John about the wet-weather plan B, he looked at me in incomprehension. 'What if it rains?' I asked. 'It's September,' he replied. 'It never rains in Santa Fe in September.'

There was also a lovely moment during the rehearsal, repeated during the service itself, when the minister (a pentecostal pastor) asked 'Who gives this woman to be married to this man?' and John replied, 'Her mother and I do.' I warmed so much to his improvised inclusiveness.

September 2017

JOYFUL CELEBRATION

We had a major fright in the small hours of the night on Friday 1 September, when Cathy became very sick. To this day, we're not sure what the problem was: whether she was reacting to something she had eaten the previous day, or to all the stress of the previous six months. But she was vomiting violently, so much so that it felt touch and go whether she would be fit enough to attend the wedding of her youngest son. It was a moment for urgent prayer! Fortunately, the wedding was not until 1pm. Cathy was still in bed at 11am, but thankfully was well enough to get up, dressed and out of our accommodation in time, albeit gingerly.

The wedding service was brief (there being no cultural tradition of congregational hymn singing on these occasions, for example), but deeply moving. It was also a stunning bit of outdoor theatre. The five bridesmaids wore black dresses with red Converse shoes; the groomsmen grey flat caps, white shirts, black trousers and black Converse; the bride a white dress and white Converse. And of course, the sun shone throughout. If we needed shelter at all, it was from the fierce sun, not any rain – unless you count my tears: I wept buckets.

The photographs were, from a Wilcox point of view, hilarious. We watched as scores of members of the bride's family assembled – perhaps 120 of them in all – gloriously multicultural and multigenerational. Then the groom's family was called, and the three of us rather sheepishly took our places: the father, mother and brother of the groom.

The reception was on the same site, in the church hall. We ate fine Mexican food, with plenty of red and green chilli, to the accompaniment of a Mariachi band. And there were four speeches, two on behalf of the groom, including a typically mischievous one by his older brother, and two on behalf of the bride – though not by her father, but by one of her sisters and one of her closest friends. The couple left the reception in an electric blue open-top Mustang, literally driving off into the sunset.

The following day we began our return journey, arriving back at Bishopscroft on the 4th. Later in the month I had planned undertake a prayer pilgrimage of the diocese, walking its length from Goole in the north east to the cathedral in the south west, covering about 70 miles in 5 days. So on Friday 8th, Cathy and I walked from Endcliffe Park in west Sheffield out into the Peak District and back, to test my strength. I was fine.

I attended my first gathering of the College of Bishops at St Hugh's College in Oxford, from 11 to 13 September. It was important to be there, even though I had not yet been installed. This was partly because of my involvement in LLF, but mostly because the Mawer report (investigating the circumstances leading to Philip North's withdrawal from the See of Sheffield) was published on the 12th. Sir Philip Mawer came to address the bishops. His report was generally affirming of those involved in the Diocese of Sheffield itself, which was a considerable relief.

The College of Bishops also allowed me my first opportunity to meet with the members of an episcopal cell group I had been invited to join. It was made up entirely of diocesan bishops, and at that time comprised the bishops of Newcastle, Ely, Chelmsford, St Edmundsbury and Ipswich, Exeter and Worcester. I was grateful for the chance to share my situation with them, confident of their prayers over the weeks ahead.

✧

Saturday 16th was a full and exciting day. There was a rehearsal at the Cathedral, a week in advance of the Service of Installation, and Tom and Rosa arrived at Bishopscroft from their honeymoon in Edinburgh.

On Monday 18th I began the prayer pilgrimage at Rawcliffe, a village outside the town of Goole in the East Riding, nearly the north-easternmost point of the Diocese. The pilgrimage was open to others, so after Morning Prayer at the parish church of St James I was joined by quite a gaggle of walkers, at least for the first few hundred yards. The crowd thinned out at Rawcliffe Bridge, as I headed out across wheatfields and moorland. The farmland was precisely one of the 'rural areas' of the Diocese which the Queen had referred to after the homage. A farmer told me that day that the East Riding of Yorkshire has one of the world's very best climates for growing wheat – but one of the very worst for harvesting it. As it happens, we were there on a dry day. Our walk also took us across the protected peat bogs of Thorne Moor, to Moorends, where we paused to pray at St Wilfrith's Church. We pressed on into the village of Thorne, where we stopped for lunch at St Nicholas Church. That afternoon we walked on to Hatfield, for a Eucharist at the Church of St Lawrence, where a goodly congregation had gathered in anticipation. I was given a lift from there back to Rawcliffe to pick up the car for the drive home.

We covered 13 miles in all on that Monday – the longest day's walking of the week. And though none of the next four days involved such a long hike, each had much the same pattern: a drive out to the previous evening's destination, walking along footpaths and pavements in the morning and afternoon, a picnic lunch and three or four prayer stations along the way. The process gave me a good taste of the breadth of theological conviction and liturgical expression in the Diocese.

I was a bit oddly dressed: hiking gear from the waist down (boots, thick socks and walking trousers); episcopal gear from the waist up (dog collar, clerical shirt, pectoral cross); plus a distinctive wooden staff which was half walking stick and half crozier. But strangers didn't seem too fazed by the sight. In fact, the curved head and neck shape at the top of the staff often prompted strangers (not least dog walkers) to remark on it, which in turn occasionally opened up substantial conversations about the 'shepherding' ministry of a bishop, and about Jesus the Good Shepherd. The only place I really turned heads, dressed the way I was, was on the final day as we walked through Meadowhall Shopping Centre on the outskirts of Sheffield. Both the hiking gear and the episcopal gear were equally out of place and the combination must have looked like some peculiar form of fancy dress.

For the sake of those of readers who know and love the communities of the East Riding and of South Yorkshire, and the incredible range of worship styles on offer in today's Church of England, our route and pattern of prayer for the rest of the week was as follows:

Tuesday: nine miles, from Hatfield to Doncaster via Edenthorpe and the Church of the Good Shepherd at Canon Popham Church of England Primary School (where my stick came into its own again), Wheatley and Doncaster Minster to the church of St James, Doncaster.

Wednesday: ten miles, from Doncaster to Conisbrough, including Mass at the traditionalist catholic parish of St Jude, Hexthorpe followed by coffee, cake and an interview at the evangelical parish of St Peter's, Conisbrough.

Thursday: ten miles, from Conisbrough to Rotherham, via the beautiful village of Ravenfield and the suburbs of St Francis of Assisi, Bramley (charismatic prayer meeting) and St Cuthbert, Herringthorpe (celtic prayers) to Rotherham Minster for a Eucharist.

Friday: the last eight miles from Rotherham Minster to Sheffield Cathedral via Wincobank, from the top of which we enjoyed panoramic views over Sheffield while we ate lunch. A Holy Communion service at St Peter's Ellesmere followed, then charismatic prayers at St Thomas Philadelphia, arriving at the Cathedral in time for Evensong.

Before that Evensong, I was presented with a new pectoral cross, which I would wear for the first time at the Service of Installation the following day. It had been specially commissioned by the Cathedral Chapter and custom made by a well-known local cutlery firm, David Mellor. In fact this piece had been personally made to my specifications by the present owner, Corin Mellor. I had asked for a simple Latin cross shape, worked in stainless steel, and heavy enough to symbolise the weight of my office.

I wear it with great pride: it locates me specifically in the Diocese of Sheffield.

The following day, Saturday 23 September, was the Installation. In the morning I noted in my journal that I was feeling in good physical health, notwithstanding the week of walking, 'a great blessing'. To my utter delight, members of the Cathedral Choir from Liverpool joined their opposite numbers in Sheffield to share in the leadership of a beautiful service, which I had worked hard to shape with the Cathedral clergy. Once again, as at the Consecration, it was overwhelming to be the focus of so much loving kindness and prayerful goodwill. Many family and friends were there, as well as good numbers from both the Diocese of Liverpool and the Diocese of Sheffield.

The service was to begin at 2pm. Around an hour before I was ensconced in a tiny attic room in the Cutlers Hall (a significant

Hallamshire institution), across the road from the main doors of the Cathedral, where I was to robe up. It was the perfect bird's eye vantage point from which I could watch the congregation arriving, praying with heartfelt gratitude for those I recognised, and asking the blessing of God on those I did not. By the time I saw robed processions filing into the Cathedral – readers and clergy from the Diocese, visiting clergy, ecumenical guests – I knew it was almost time for me to be collected and led across to the Cathedral.

Such services traditionally begin with a ritual in which the new bishop requests entrance by banging three times on the Great West Door of the Cathedral with a pastoral staff. In Sheffield, this required a bit of ingenuity, since the doors are glass. The vergers had found a solution, fixing a block of wood at an appropriate height. I could bang it as hard as I wished and be heard inside the Cathedral, with no risk of smashing anything.

Then we were underway. The first person to speak was a primary school child, who asked me in whose name and in what spirit I had come. 'In the name of Christ, and Christ crucified,' I replied. Then I was granted entrance and made my way slowly up the nave aisle as the choir sang 'I Was Glad' by Parry. I processed in rather simply robed. In the course of the next hour, I was gradually clothed in the symbolic vestments of the Diocesan Bishop: stole, cope and mitre – and the official Diocesan crozier to replace my wooden staff. I was anointed, and then placed in the 'cathedra', the official seat of the bishop in the Cathedral Church. And along the way, I had the opportunity to preach. I had chosen the opening nine verses of 2 Corinthians 8 – which allowed me to speak about generosity as a Christian virtue. The text of the sermon is included at the end of this book on page 117.

No sooner was the Installation behind us than Cathy and I found ourselves gearing up for another major celebration a week later: the Service of Wedding Blessing for Tom and Rosa on Saturday 30th. In between, both Cathy and I had other commitments to negotiate.

Many, many months previously, when we had no idea this week would be book-ended by these two great celebration services, Cathy had accepted an invitation to address the Diocese of Worcester Clergy Conference at the Hayes Conference Centre in Swanwick. As such, she was away overnight on Wednesday 27th, just as Rosa's parents and two of her sisters arrived at Manchester airport. Similarly, many months previously, I had accepted an invitation from Bishop Paul Bayes to lead a clergy study day for the Diocese of Liverpool on the Book of Ruth that same day. And on the Thursday, I had my hospital appointment for CT and MRI scans. Once again, it was the 'yanking' of my emotions, from anxiety over the cancer, to joy at family and vocational developments, to routine ministerial engagements, which I found most difficult to deal with.

So the month ended very much as it began – only this time, the Wilcox clan was present in greater numbers, with only five Griegos able to make the trip from New Mexico. We had erected a marquee capable of accommodating 90 on the lawn at Bishopscroft – because unlike Santa Fe, you can't guarantee there will be no rain in Sheffield in September. And sure enough, we were glad of the cover! It was mostly dry, but we didn't escape the odd shower. Afterwards, the guests were served fish and chips from one van, and ice cream from another.

October 2017

SETTLING IN

On Sunday 1 October it was my privilege to preach and preside at the Cathedral's 10.30am Choral Eucharist, and the following day members of Rosa's family left to return to Santa Fe.

If September was dominated by celebration services, personal and vocational, October was dominated by the prospect of surgery. The consultation I attended on the 5th made it clear that, while the chemoradiotherapy had been extremely effective in reducing the mass of the tumour, I definitely still required surgery and that might quite possibly be followed by further post-op preventative chemo. I was warned that a colostomy might be necessary, given the site of the tumour, but was told that decision would be made by the surgeon when I met with him the following week.

In between those two appointments, on Saturday 7 October, came the Diocesan Development Day. These annual occasions are gatherings of over 300 clergy and key lay leaders from across the Diocese, for equipping and envisioning through plenary sessions and workshops. It was my responsibility to deliver a keynote address first thing in the morning and since this was my very first opportunity to address the Diocese 'at large'. I was desperately keen to make a positive impression. I wanted to set out my stall as a Bible teacher, with a heart both for evangelism, and for the poor and those on the margins of our society. Thus, it was an obvious decision for me to offer an exposition of the Gospel of Luke: the good news of Jesus, the saviour of the whole world, including those on the outside.

The meeting with the surgeon took place on 10 October, which happened to be my 56th birthday. As a result of that consultation I noted in my journal, 'I'm pretty confident of seeing my 60th, though there's major surgery to contend with in the next few weeks.'

The operation was scheduled for All Saints' Day, 1 November, and the surgeon confirmed that a colostomy would indeed be necessary. That came, as I noted in my journal, as quite a 'numbing blow'. A bit of online research in the following days wasn't altogether reassuring – some accounts indicated a significant change in lifestyle. I had initially been encouraged to suppose the lifestyle implications were minimal. At this point, I was less sure.

A firm date for the surgery was a significant development. Until then, it had all felt a little unreal and theoretical. Now the reality was inescapable: it required some significant rejigging of the diary. Again, this was a moment in which I'm aware I prioritised my own needs and those of the diocese over the needs of my nearest and dearest, including Cathy. I more or less presented her with a fait accompli, that I would have the operation as far as possible under the radar. To my regret, I don't recall asking her what she would prefer. I therefore gave my PA the unenviable task of presenting my apologies for a whole series of appointments which had been agreed for the first two weeks of November. Chief among these was a church wardens' conference scheduled for Saturday 4 November. Church wardens are among the most valuable and hard-pressed volunteers in the Church of England, and I had been very keen to affirm their ministries by attending the conference that day. Instead, they had to make do with an address recorded on video, and my profound apologies –and a commitment to attend the following year. Not for the last time, I think we resorted to that time-honoured phrase and attributed my withdrawal, at relatively short notice, to 'unforeseen circumstances'.

Meanwhile, my public ministry was underway and on Wednesday 11th I licensed a new minister for the first time. As it happens, he was a Methodist minister, serving a Local Ecumenical Partnership. It wasn't quite an 'ordinary' commissioning service – but since he would have the 'cure of souls' for the Anglicans in that parish, the minister did require my licence. In an ecumenical service, the anachronistic legal language in which clergy licences are couched sounds even more clunky than usual. Matters were not helped on this occasion by the fact that where I was supposed to say, 'Peter Jonathan, by Divine Permission, Lord Bishop of Sheffield,' I managed to say, 'Peter Jonathan, by Divine Permission, Lord Bishop of Liverpool.' There may be an unhelpful culture of deference in some parts of the Church of England, but it was immediately clear that congregations in South Yorkshire would have no difficulty enjoying a chuckle at my expense.

I was back to the hospital on the 17th for a pre-op assessment. It involved being weighed and measured, having my pulse and blood pressure checked and an ECG and my 'bloods' done. A kindly nurse also marked up the site for the colostomy, to guide the surgeon. I remember looking at the mark over the course of the following fortnight, viewing it as a bit of an unwelcome intruder.

Towards the end of the month I was able to take a few days of annual leave. It was an opportunity to visit my parents in Eastbourne and my oldest son in Bristol and to provide them with a face-to-face update on what lay ahead. Rightly or wrongly I chose not to tell my parents at that point about the likelihood of a colostomy.

On the very last day of the month, and on the eve of the surgery, I drove with a colleague to Whitehaven in the Diocese of Carlisle, to meet with clergy leaders there in advance of an ecumenical bishops' mission planned for March 2018. It was a bit surreal to drive the three hours there and three hours back, for a two-hour planning meeting, knowing what I would face the very next morning. The feeling was compounded by the fact that on that very day, while I was still in the Lake District, my official episcopal car was finally delivered, almost five months after it was first due. Ironically, the surgery meant I would be unable to drive it for at least a fortnight, and probably longer!

November 2017

UNDERGOING SURGERY

The Five Transactional Analysis Drivers identified by Taibi Kahler (Kahler's Drivers), are a tool both Cathy and I have both found very useful in understanding ourselves, our motivations, choices and responses. The five drivers are: Be Perfect, Be Strong, Hurry Up, Please People and Try Harder. Most people seem to recognise that one or two of these 'drive' them. In Cathy's case, it's Be Perfect and Please People: she herself offers the suggestion that her desire to please me may have led her to downplay her own needs at various points of this year when we were making choices about how to cope with our situation. My drivers are without question Hurry Up and Be Strong, and in responding to the surgery as I did during November 2017, I was simply coping in the best way I knew. I was driven.

All Saints' Day is celebrated on 1 November each year. It is a much-cherished day in the Christian calendar, when we recall our solidarity with the baptised in every time and place. Christians form one body of Christ: we are one with all who have gone before us, one with all who will come after us, and one with all who serve the Lord Jesus in the present time, in any and every part of the world. In 2017, the date was full of resonance for me. I was very aware of the relatively small but precious band of Christians, mostly in the UK but also scattered around the world, who were praying for me. And I was aware of my mortality and the certain fact of my death: that at some point I would join those who 'have gone before us in the faith of Christ'.

It was also almost a year to the day since I heard that I had been called to interview by the CNC for the Sheffield post. That twelve months had turned out to be a monster of a rollercoaster ride – and it wasn't finished yet.

It was an early start. We left the house at 6.30am to ensure we were at the Northern General Hospital in Sheffield as required by 7.00. We were in good time. Cathy and I shared a hug and a kiss before she drove away and I reported in at the theatre admissions unit. There was inevitably a good deal of anxious waiting, but eventually I was called.

I have never been very good with blood and gore, particularly in medical settings. It didn't seem to affect me in the same way on a rugby pitch, back in the day. But I fainted in the delivery room when our first son was on the way, taking out an expensive piece of medical equipment as I fell. And on this occasion too I fainted as an epidural was administered.

The next thing I knew, I was being wheeled back from theatre to a recovery ward and from there (thank the Lord!), to a single room. Privacy meant a great deal to me in the next few days. The surgery had lasted eight hours. I was of course oblivious to the passage of time – but Cathy was not. It speaks volumes for the quality of care we received that the surgeon phoned her in person after the operation was over, to let her know it had been a success. Cathy came into the hospital on the evening of the operation. I thought I was pretty clear-headed already and functioning well, but she just laughs when I tell her so. Apparently, I wasn't making much sense at all at that point.

The surgeon popped in to see me the following day, as did his assistant. The surgeon was confident he had 'got the lot'. He told me he had taken out a slice of my coccyx and a slice of my prostate just to be absolutely sure. Separately, his assistant told me she was equally confident the prospects for the histology were good.

I was feeling quite alert: able to read and even to do a few emails – though there is no journal entry on Thursday 2 November. However, I had lost the feeling in my right leg, which was also becoming quite swollen and was worrying me. The acute pain specialist was also concerned about this, but the situation was resolved as soon as they removed the epidural. Otherwise, there was no sign of any complications.

The operation had indeed left me with a permanent colostomy. I remember feeling around my abdomen when I first regained consciousness to establish what was there and finding a bag. I am the sort of person who much prefers to have all the information, even when there is bad news, so that I can begin to adapt to the future accordingly. In this case, I had been given plenty of warning that this was a likely outcome, so it was hardly a shock – and when the stoma nurse called, I was eager to take control of my new situation as fully and quickly as possible. She was outstanding in explaining how I would need to manage bag-changes and what options might be open to me longer term. Cathy and I quickly took to calling the colostomy 'Eglon' after the Moabite king of that name in Judges 3. Readers for whom the reference is unfamiliar may enjoy looking it up.

Over the next few days, pain management became easier. There was one frightening episode, however. One night, in my sleep, I managed to dislodge a canula and woke to discover that the bed was soaked in blood. A nurse came swiftly when I called and she immediately identified and rectified the problem, and changed the bed-linen and my pyjamas, so that I was able to return to sleep surprisingly quickly.

Meanwhile, I had been told before the operation that 'highly motivated' patients are sometimes discharged within a few days, and I told the nursing staff I was probably about as highly motivated as a patient could be. Sure enough, the consultant approved my discharge on Sunday 5 November, after the catheter had been removed and I was able to demonstrate that my plumbing was all in working order.

I left with what felt like a lorry load of kit: various sizes and styles of stoma pouches, wet wipes and dry wipes, deodorant and adhesive removal sprays, disposal bags, various kinds of pain relief, syringes for the daily injections I would have to administer myself to the thigh to prevent blood clots, and a sharps box for used syringes. Cathy came to collect me, with Neil our gardener/driver. I was just about able, with support, to walk upright to the car – but only just. And when we got back to Bishopscroft, I went straight to bed and remained there for a couple of days.

On Tuesday 7 November, I managed to get dressed for the first time and to take a short walk in the garden. I spoke to the surgeon on the phone, who urged me to keep a particular eye on the wound in my rear end – an infection there was apparently the most likely complication. In the following days, I had low-level aching pain in my abdomen and rear, and my concentration levels were low. On the Wednesday a follow-up call with nurses on the colorectal team provided a reality check: recovery was a long game. Yet very few people seemed to notice how invisible I was that November – perhaps because everyone was assuming that the new bishop was busy in some other part of the Diocese.

On Thursday 9th the surgeon phoned again, this time to tell me the histology results, which were excellent – as good as could be, he said. In shorthand, the histology was T0N2. That meant that the primary tumour (T) had in fact been destroyed (0) by the chemoradiotherapy during the summer (bye bye Lucille). And of 13 secondary nodes (N) which had been identified before that treatment took place, only 2 had survived, and both of them had been successfully removed. The Lord be blessed and praised!

On Tuesday 14th my GP cleared me to drive, and I managed 6,000 paces on a walk around the block for the first time since the surgery. 'Everything still feels as if it's healing up nicely,' I noted. Two days later I was back in a dog collar for my first piece of public ministry since the operation. It was the Church Burgesses rent audit dinner at the Cutlers' Hall. The Church Burgesses are a venerable Sheffield charity, managing historic assets in support of the mission of the church. Their dinner is an annual occasion, now geared to expressing the gratitude of the Burgesses to their friends and partners. It was my first such dinner and I was glad to be there. I was in no pain, but I was a bit nervous about Eglon's first outing. In fact, everything was fine, and I can't imagine anyone there had any idea about my situation, though they may have found the new Bishop of Sheffield a bit lacking in sparkle!

A few days later, Cathy and I travelled back to Liverpool overnight to visit our good friend there, Kate Wharton. Kate is a priest, and she is single, having embraced that state as her calling. Two years previously, we had attended a bespoke evening service in the chapel at Bishop's Lodge in Liverpool, presided over by Bishop Paul Bayes, at which Kate had entered a sort of 'novitiate': a two-year period of testing, to establish if she truly wished to make vows of singleness and celibacy. At that service, Kate informally nominated Cathy and me as her 'Guardians of the Vow'.

Two years on, on Saturday 18 November, Kate was ready to make those lifelong promises before God and I was desperately keen to be at her 'Beloved' ceremony in the Lady Chapel of Liverpool Cathedral if at all possible. Indeed, Kate had invited me to preach. Thank God, it proved manageable – only an entirely straightforward recovery could have enabled that.

I was back at the Northern General Hospital on Tuesday 21st for a follow-up consultation with the surgeon and the lead nurse on the colorectal nurses team. They examined my wounds and gave an encouraging report. They even cleared me to resume jogging as soon as I felt strong enough. The surgeon did warn me of the risk of 'chafing' when running, but I didn't really grasp what he meant. He also talked me through my options with regard to post-op chemo and encouraged me to take advantage of the opportunity. I noted in my journal at the time what I assume I was told on that day: that there was a 30% risk of a recurrence of the disease during the first 2 years after the operation, but that a course of chemotherapy would reduce that to around 25%.

I wasn't particularly keen to commit to that path. It would mean considerable diary adjustments for the first three months of 2018. I also felt that I would then need to maintain secrecy about the treatment and my situation for a further period. By now I was looking forward to beginning a regime for managing the colostomy known as 'irrigation' – a daily routine of flushing out the colon to eliminate additional, unpredictable bowel movements. I was keen to experiment with that system as I was very attracted by the degree of control it offered. But irrigation is not compatible with chemotherapy, so a further course of treatment would delay that step. On the other hand, it was put to me that accepting a further course of chemo would enable me to contribute to clinical trials. After all the benefits I had received from the NHS free of charge, it was hard to turn down an opportunity to give something back. On that basis I agreed to a three-month course of intravenous chemotherapy, to begin in the New Year.

I was back in Liverpool and at the Cathedral once more on Thursday 24 November for a graduation ceremony for Liverpool John Moores University. The University had generously made me a Fellow in recognition of my civic ministry during my tenure as Dean. It was a great honour – but I now know that after colorectal surgery the last thing a person needs is to be seated on a hard chair on a podium for hours on end! I was so sore afterwards.

✧

On Saturday 25th I attended my first meeting of the Diocesan Synod in Sheffield. I had invited Sir Philip Mawer to address the Synod and to interpret his report for us. Both his presentation and his responses to questions were clear and skilful, and I felt he gave much-needed reassurance to those present. But it probably speaks volumes about my state of mind and my nervousness at set-piece public engagements that my journal entry has nothing to do with the effectiveness of Sir Philip's contribution, or even to do with the reception for my own first presidential address. I simply noted, 'That's one more public event at which I was not embarrassed by my stoma.'

It's a mark of how well my recovery had gone that on Monday 27th, Cathy and I attempted a short run together: just a gentle jog in a nearby park, barely a mile and a half.

Unfortunately, two days later, after almost three weeks of consistent (if gradual) improvement, I found myself in severe pain. 'I've definitely picked up some sort of infection,' I wrote. And the following day, 'It's inflamed and very sore down below.' The surgeon had warned me this was a real danger and now I could see why. I made an appointment to see the GP and she prescribed antibiotics.

Meanwhile, on the final day of the month I had an appointment with the consultant who would be arranging the chemotherapy. He recommended three cycles of three weeks each, with a week off between each cycle. Each cycle was to begin with one day of intravenous chemotherapy, followed by a regime of tablets for the remainder of the three weeks. It wasn't what I would have chosen, but I resolved to begin the process. The consultant stressed that there would be the option of 'bailing out' after each of the first two cycles, if the toll was too great. Of the three, the first cycle would be disproportionately effective in any case.

December 2017

LOOKING BACK

The following day, Friday 1 December, I was still getting no relief from the antibiotics I had begun taking. 'I'm in as much pain this morning as in the past two days,' I noted. The next day I wrote, 'I'm still in some pain, but perhaps not as much as I was on each of the past four mornings, so maybe the antibiotics are beginning to take effect.'

I admit, I was a little slow on the uptake. It was only on the next day, which happened to be Advent Sunday, that I realised the real problem. There was no infection at all. It was the jogging which had caused the inflammation: the wound in my backside was chafing, which the surgeon had warned me about. All that was required was a rest from jogging.

That Advent Sunday was especially memorable. First, in the morning, it was my privilege to preside for the first time at a Confirmation Service at the Rivers Team in Rotherham. This included 3 baptisms by immersion (in a birthing pool brought into the church specifically for the purpose), and 15 candidates for confirmation, young people and adults and from a glorious diversity of backgrounds.

Every bishop I know finds confirmation services to be among the greatest privileges of episcopal ministry. It's always a joy to meet the candidates before the service and to hear a little about the journey of faith which has brought them to the point of wanting publicly to align their lives with the life, death and resurrection of Jesus. The testimonies are often deeply moving. In the past six years, I have continued to prioritise the chance to talk with candidates – they almost invariably renew my own faith.

Then in the evening, I attended the Advent Carol Service at Sheffield Cathedral for the first time. Inevitably, I found myself thinking back to the service in Liverpool twelve months before.

It had been a remarkable year. I'm not sure how I would have coped had I known on Advent Sunday 2016 what the coming months would bring. And yet – and yet strength was given for each day, and moments of hope and even joy in the process. That twelve-month period is not by any means an experience I would have chosen. And yet I can say that on the evening of Advent Sunday 2017, my heart was full of thanksgiving. I had in fact experienced this as 'a year of the Lord's favour.'

Since I was a young teenager, my 'compass north' has been my sense of myself in relation to Jesus, my Saviour and Master. I can identify with the saying attributed to St Polycarp on the day of his death, 'Eighty and six years have I served [Jesus], and he has done me no wrong.'

Similarly, I love the song, composed in 1971 by Gavin Bryars and based on the testimony of a homeless man, 'Jesus' blood never failed me yet'. This is my experience. In seeking to live out my life in the service of Christ Jesus, I have never felt let down by him. On the contrary, it has been a rich and glorious experience – and I would include in that description the period recorded in this memoir.

I can't swear that the traditional 18th century poem, 'Jesus Christ, the Apple Tree' was sung by the choir at that service, but it almost certainly was. It sums up beautifully how I was feeling, one year on.

The Tree of Life my soul hath seen,
Laden with fruit and always green;
The trees of nature fruitless be,
Compared with Christ the Apple Tree.

His beauty doth all things excel,
By faith I know but ne'er can tell
The glory which I now can see,
In Jesus Christ the Appletree.

For happiness I long have sought,
And pleasure dearly I have bought;
I missed of all but now I see
'Tis found in Christ the Appletree.

I'm weary with my former toil –
Here I will sit and rest awhile,
Under the shadow I will be,
Of Jesus Christ the Appletree.

This fruit doth make my soul to thrive,
It keeps my dying faith alive;
Which makes my soul in haste to be
With Jesus Christ the Appletree.

POSTSCRIPT

I did duly embark on some post-operative chemotherapy in early 2018, but it was not for me. I found my first session of intravenous treatment far more debilitating than I had anticipated, and my aversion to the large pink chemo tablets had only increased since the summer. After only a few days, I was feeling so dreadful that I wrote to the consultant to withdraw from the process. He was entirely understanding.

One benefit of that decision was that three months after that single session of chemotherapy, I was able to begin a routine of irrigation which has stood me in good stead ever since. The process is quite demanding in terms of time and space: it often takes me 45 minutes or so to complete. Days that always required an early start now require a very early start! I have become a connoisseur of bathroom layouts, rejoicing when there are ample ledges on which I can lay out all the necessary paraphernalia. But the effort required to irrigate is well worthwhile: most days it means Eglon is then entirely inactive, and my colostomy bag sits empty, serving only as a precautionary measure.

The result, in my case, is that a colostomy has not been particularly life-diminishing. It does not restrict my capacity for physical exercise, for example – only my advancing age does that. So far, it has not embarrassed me significantly in public – only my inherent folly does that. It does mean I am uncomfortable using a shared bathroom, but I observe that most people of my age prefer the convenience of an en suite! It does also mean that I now have to give some extra thought to overnight stays away from home and to trips abroad: I have had to learn the hard way to remember to pack everything I need, with quantities to spare. It is, of course, a great blessing that the considerable volume of 'colostomy kit' I use comes free of charge thanks to the NHS. Every month I take delivery of a box of bits and pieces to order, and so far the process has, thankfully, proved consistently reliable.

During the first two years after the surgery, in which the risk of a recurrence of the disease was at its greatest, I was monitored very closely by the colorectal department at the Northern General Hospital. Every three months I underwent a scan or test, including two follow-up colonoscopy examinations. After the first two years, the monitoring became more light touch. Every three months, and later every six months, I would visit the hospital to provide a blood sample, which would be tested for my CEA (carcinoembryonic antigen) level. A rising CEA score is one early sign that cancer has returned to the body. My scores were consistently normal.

Inevitably, Cathy and I worried a good deal about the prospect of a return of the cancer, especially in the first couple of years. In 2018 and 2019, we marked 1 November as a significant and life-giving anniversary. Our 'deal' was that in alternate years, each of us would organise a surprise visit for the other on that date. In 2018, it meant that at Cathy's design, we spent 1 November at Crich Tram Museum. In 2019, we went to the theatre. Neither of those two events was a conspicuous success (for which the venues bear no fault) and we abandoned the routine after just two years!

One incident from that time comes to mind: one morning I discovered that there was bleeding from my stoma. It seemed clear to me that this meant the cancer had returned. I didn't tell Cathy, but I made an urgent phonecall to the colorectal department of the hospital. Almost at once, I detected not anxiety but puzzlement in the nurse to whom I was speaking. She said, 'Is there anything else which has been different?' 'Well,' I said, 'I did misjudge the temperature of the water I introduced in irrigation yesterday. I may have scalded myself.' At that point, I heard the nurse laugh out loud. 'That would do it,' she said.

Five years on, those who have been through colorectal surgery are no longer meaningfully at additional risk of a recurrence of the disease – so in late October 2022, I was discharged from the Northern General Hospital. It was that landmark which finally enabled me, in a presidential address to the Diocesan Synod the following month, to put this story on the record (see page 102).

I am so grateful to those whose support has enabled me to make this journey. As I tried to convey in that presidential address, I simply could not have survived my illness without others: in many parts of the world, in most centuries before now, this illness would have been fatal. Without free access to considerable medical research, equipment, expertise and skill, I would not have survived. I am especially grateful to those who diagnosed the problem; to those who devised a treatment plan; to those who delivered the chemotherapy and radiotherapy; to those who operated on me; and to those who, over the course of the past five years, have checked up on me with tests every few months to make sure all is well. It is particularly worth stating that Sheffield NHS Teaching Hospitals Trust is a world-class institution – and I have seen it at first hand.

I am also grateful to those who have supported me in other ways: to colleagues in Liverpool and Sheffield who have borne with me, prayed for me and kept confidences. I am of course grateful to God for his grace and manifold blessings. Grace is sometimes defined as 'God's undeserved favour'. It is in that sense that I look back on this twelve-month period as 'a year of the LORD's favour' – not only because the illness was not fatal in my case, but because it has formed me in ways that have been good for me.

Of course, it is ultimately for others to judge. But I sense the experience has made me more tolerant of the limitations and shortcomings of others. I am more grateful for the life I have been given, more aware of the value of each day, and it has made me more appreciative of the help and support I receive from others. In other words, it has made me more aware of my own weakness and dependency, and of my mortality. Thanks be to God.

As well as the Methodist Covenant Prayer, throughout the past five years there is another prayer which has been a constant source of encouragement to me, and which I have used often. It is sometimes called the 'Lutheran prayer for courage' and I hope it might be as much of a help to some of the readers of these pages as it has been to me.

> Lord God,
> you have called your servants to ventures of which we
>   cannot see the ending,
> by paths as yet untrodden, through perils unknown.
> Give us faith to go out with good courage, not knowing
>   where we go,
> but only that your hand is leading us and your love
>   supporting us;
> through Jesus Christ our Lord. Amen.

ACKNOWLEDGEMENTS

In November 2016, I was Dean of Liverpool. I would like to express my thanks and appreciation to the colleagues, lay and ordained, with whom I was working at that time, and especially to the members of the Cathedral Chapter, for their love and support, their prayers and tenderness during my entire tenure in that post, but especially over the course of the following year. Twelve months on, I was the Bishop of Sheffield. During 2017, colleagues in the Diocese, especially on the bishop's senior staff team, had to cope with the arrival of a second-choice new bishop, who at once confided in them his need for treatment, including surgery, for cancer. I want to pay tribute to them for their fortitude and unflappability, their concern and kindness in the face of a challenging situation. Perhaps unfairly, I asked them to keep my illness confidential and as far as I can tell they did so with commendable rigour.

I was blessed with extraordinary medical care: from Dr Angus Blair, now retired, who was then the Church of England's 'go-to' doctor for medical examinations on Harley Street; from Mr Al Windsor, a colorectal specialist consultant who worked in the same practice; and later from the staff of Weston Park Hospital and the Northern General Hospital, both part of Sheffield Teaching Hospitals NHS Trust, whose professionalism and skill was consistently coupled with exemplary courtesy and pastoral care for which I am deeply grateful. In the early stages of the diagnosis I made repeated trips to London and was offered typically generous hospitality by Andy and Caroline Brookes, whose friendship over the decades has been a great gift to Cathy and me, which grows more precious over time.

Other friends and family members, including my theological cell group and my episcopal cell group, along with my spiritual director, prayed for me and cared for me through that year. Without that undergirding, I doubt I could have endured the experience.

The heaviest burdens were inevitably borne by my closest family: my parents and siblings, and my sons and daughters-in-law (Jon and Izzy, Tom and Rosa). But the heaviest burden of all was borne by Cathy, my dearest earthly love, whose wit is equal to every crisis, whose faithfulness is great, and whose mercies (like her Saviour's) are new every morning.

PRESIDENTIAL ADDRESS TO SHEFFIELD DIOCESE SYNOD

November 2022

My dear friends, it's the Eve of Advent, a season I love. I love the strong liturgical backdrop we will enjoy for the next four weeks; I love the Advent hymns; I love the sense of anticipation and expectation. I love the sustained and deliberate focus, in this season of joyful hope, on the assurance of God's coming kingdom.

But today, I want to look back and not forward, and I want to offer you a presidential address with a difference. This morning I want to speak very personally – to tell you about a particular health challenge I have had to face over the past five years. It's basically a good news story, though I realise the new information may be a bit unsettling for some of you.

To cut to the chase: about four weeks ago, at the start of the month, I was, thank God, signed off by the colorectal department at the Northern General Hospital, because it is five years since I went through treatment for cancer of the colon, and I am no longer meaningfully at risk of a recurrence of the disease. This morning, I'd like to tell you about the diagnosis and treatment I experienced in 2017, and about the impact it has had on me as a person and as a bishop.

I realise this raises questions. Some of you may be wondering why I did not tell you about this at the time, in 2017? It's a fair point. I do know that you would have been only too keen to pray for me and to care for me pastorally if you had known what I was going through back then. So why didn't I tell you? Well, partly, I was simply protecting myself. I'm an extreme introvert and in that situation I needed some privacy. But in addition, in mid 2017, this Diocese had just emerged from a torrid Vacancy in See. By then, though I myself was pretty confident, on medical advice, that the prognosis was good, though I was pretty confident of being Bishop of Sheffield long-term, given what many of you had recently gone through, I was concerned that news of my illness might create additional instability, and I thought that was the last thing this Diocese needed. So I chose not to go public.

But let me assure you, I did not endure the experience heroically alone. I needed support and I received it. I told those who were back then members of the Bishop's senior staff team, and those who were on staff at Bishopscroft. I told the members of my theological college cell group and the members of my episcopal cell group; I told colleagues I was just in the process of leaving in Liverpool; and I told other close friends and family members. All of them duly prayed for me and cared for me. So please be assured that I did not go through the experience I am about to describe on my own; I could not have done so.

Others of you may be wondering, why I am telling you now? Is it because at this point the vulnerability is over, so I can now present a conquering face to you all? No, as I will explain in a moment, it's really not that. Quite the contrary in fact. But the five-year anniversary since the surgery does give me an opportunity to tell this story without making you worry about the risk of recurrence; and it allows me to put the story on the record in a reasonably full and careful way. And I think that might be valuable, so let me try.

And yes, as you may already have worked out, I was dealing with the diagnosis and treatment in exactly the period in which I was taking up my responsibilities as Bishop of Sheffield. In fact, that's partly why I am choosing to tell you this story today, because my cancer was integral to my sense of calling to this role.

Every new bishop is offered a medical, and when the Archbishop of York offered me the opportunity, in early March 2017, to accept this post, I underwent one later that month. And it was basically fine.

It did throw up a question about my prostate, but that's not unusual in men of my age and is generally not life-threatening, and a preliminary scan seemed reassuring.

So the announcement of my appointment went ahead on Friday 7 April, two days before Palm Sunday 2017. The next day, on the way home to Liverpool, with the news of my appointment now out in the open after we had kept it confidential for a month, Cathy and I had lunch at a pub in the Peak District, to celebrate that the worst was behind us. How wrong we were! Merely as a precaution, a follow-up colonoscopy had been scheduled five days later, on the Wednesday of Holy Week. That procedure was only minutes underway when the atmosphere in the operating theatre changed and I knew I was in trouble. The consultant found a tumour.

For a period of a week, I knew I had cancer, but I did not know the extent, or how treatable it might be. That week included Maundy Thursday, Good Friday, Holy Saturday and Easter Day. You can imagine, I'm sure, that it was a difficult few days for Cathy and me as we sought to surrender ourselves fully to Lord's good will and purpose. There were lots of tears – for me especially when I was breaking the news to our two sons, and to my elderly parents. But to our delight, Cathy and I found that there was also an intense sense of the presence of God with us, and of gratitude: gratitude for the gift of life; for faith and hope and love. A pivotal moment came on Good Friday, when a colleague in Liverpool stressed in a homily the role in our Lord's passion of Simon of Cyrene. He pointed out that even the Lord needed others to help him bear his burdens and we should be prepared to seek help too. That provoked Cathy and me to ask for support, when otherwise I at least might indeed have been tempted to go it alone.

Happily, the following week, a head to toe scan showed that the cancer was confined to my colon. Unfortunately, it also showed that, as well as chemoradiotherapy, surgery would be necessary, which would almost certainly result in a permanent colostomy and a new regime for disposing of waste. But the consultant was speaking about a cure, and when I sought the Lord, I sensed he was saying that this illness was not raising the question whether I would be the Bishop of Sheffield; it was raising the question, what sort of bishop I would be.

The next six months were hard, I have to confess. We moved house in mid June 2017, and I was consecrated as a bishop on the 22nd. I kid you not, but during the actual service at York Minster, I felt the phone buzz in my pocket and as I walked from the service to a reception afterwards, I listened to a voicemail from Weston Park Hospital, informing me that a five-week course of chemoradiotherapy had been scheduled. So from late June to the end of July that year, I made almost daily visits to Weston Park for radiotherapy, and I was taking chemo tablets. It was fine at first, but cumulatively tough, and by the end of July I was pretty feeble. Yet by God's grace, I went through that hard slog in the period between my consecration and my installation, when I could and did pace myself, when I could and did take time out to rest and recuperate.

August and early September were an especially timely opportunity for respite and by the grace of God I recovered enough health and strength to mean that in the week before I was installed, in late September, I was fit enough to walk from Rawcliffe, near Goole, to the Cathedral, on a prayer pilgrimage.

Five weeks after that memorable, wonderful Service of Installation, I was admitted to the Northern General for surgery, which was, thank God, entirely successful. As anticipated, however, it did leave me with a permanent colostomy. Very few people seemed to notice how invisible I was that November – perhaps because everyone was assuming that the new bishop was busy in some other part of the Diocese. As a matter of fact, I was out of action for about a month. Thankfully, since then, every single test, scan and investigation has issued in a positive result and I have felt as fit and well as any man aged 60 plus has any right to feel.

So, why am I telling you all this now? I suppose there are four reasons.

The first is this: not every vulnerability, not every disability, is visible. I know that I am a person of extreme privilege, who can appear to take life in his stride, as if it is all too easy. It's important that you know that that is not the case. If I appear to some of you to be quite self-sufficient, it's good that you know how aware I am of my dependence on others. That was a key lesson for me in the six months between April and November 2017. I was acutely dependent on others, and that experience has had a lasting impact on me. I depended on the skill and expertise of many other people, mostly medics. I depended on those who diagnosed the problem; on those who devised a treatment plan; on those who delivered the chemotherapy and radiotherapy; on those who operated on me; and for the past five years I have depended on those who have checked up on me with tests every few months to make sure all is well. And equally, I have depended on those who have made this journey with me, loving me and praying for me. Without others, I could not have come through this experience.

So when at the time of my greatest uncertainty, in Holy Week 2017, I was urgently seeking the Lord about his good will and purpose for me (when I sensed that he was saying, 'This is not a question of whether you will be the Bishop of Sheffield, this is a question of the sort of bishop you will be') this is what I took the Lord to mean: that as a bishop I would not be self sufficient, but would be dependent on the expertise and skill of others, and dependent on the prayers and support of others; that I could not come through this experience, the experience of episcopacy, without others. I have embraced that calling gladly. As your bishop, I am not independent, I am not self-sufficient, I know my need of others, and that includes you.

Secondly, in a funny way, I sensed that the challenge posed by the cancer was somehow preparatory for the challenges I would face in this ministry. I came to Sheffield after a five-year period as Dean of Liverpool which was extraordinarily fruitful. For a whole host of reasons, very few of which I had any actual control over, virtually everything my colleagues and I attempted there during that time seemed to burst at once into extravagant bloom. It was glorious – but it was not normal in Christian ministry. Of course, I had no idea about the pandemic, nor even about the full extent of the financial challenges which lay in store here, but I did sense that in Sheffield I would have to dig deeper, and toil harder for fruit – and the cancer somehow became a symbol of that, almost the word of the Lord to me. My colostomy has become for me a bit like Jacob's limp, if you recall that story in Genesis 32, a daily reminder to me that life with God is often a struggle, more like a wrestling match than a stroll in the park. Ministry can be hard going.

Thirdly, I am telling you because a colostomy has an unhelpful and unnecessary stigma, and I hope that being open about my situation might help and encourage others. This, by the way, is one reason why I like to wear a waistcoat. Like this, there is no bulge. I look almost trim. Now, every person is different, and not everyone with a colostomy can say this, but as a matter of fact, my condition has not restricted me significantly. It has required me to adopt a new routine at the start of each day, which is a bit fiddly and time-consuming, which (for someone like me who tends to live life in a hurry) can be a tad frustrating. But if I can only jog slowly round Damflask, that's on account of my dodgy knees, not the colostomy. If I can only hack my way comically around a golf course, that's on account of my dodgy technique, not the colostomy. And so on. I can still swim, and kayak, and climb hills, and the physical limitations I do encounter these days when I try to exert my body are really just a reflection of my age. In my case a colostomy has not been a serious impediment to the fulness of life and I thought that might be worth saying.

And finally, I am telling you because in all this I have known the Lord's goodness. I do believe this experience has refined me, spiritually. Some of you are aware that I literally number my days. Today, for example, is the 22,327th day of my life. I began this discipline in the header of my daily prayer journal in Holy Week 2017, when I was acutely aware there might not be many days left to my life. I certainly wasn't sure there would be 21,000. By God's grace, there have now been over 22,000 days of my life. But I am still daily aware of my mortality, daily aware that the number of my days is limited. One day, there will be a death date to go with my birth date, and in between will be the number of my days. For now, I don't know what that number is, but because they are limited, I am determined to make the most of every one, and my illness has really helped to do that. It has helped me to savour every good thing the Lord has given me and to take nothing for granted. It has helped me to see every day more clearly in the light of eternity and to live each day unto the Lord. It has helped me to thank God for each day. My illness has been good for me.

Dear friends, there we have it. I do hope I have pitched this address in a way which is helpful to you. I want you to know that I have in fact been sustained by your encouragement and support in this ministry right from day one, even though many of you were not aware of what I was going through at that time. It has been and it remains the greatest privilege of my life to be the Bishop of Sheffield and if the Lord grants me health and strength I hope to remain so for almost another decade.

So I am grateful for all the ways in which you sustain me. But you won't be surprised to know that I have also been sustained in the past five years by the daily reading of scripture, and not least by Psalm 130.

As it happens, the passage has a nice Advent resonance, so as I conclude, let me read it now.

> Out of the depths I cry to you, O Lord. Lord, hear my voice!
> Let your ears be attentive to the voice of my supplications!
> If you, O Lord, should mark iniquities, Lord, who could stand?
> But there is forgiveness with you, so that you may be revered.
> I wait for the Lord; my soul waits, and in his word I hope;
> my soul waits for the Lord
> more than those who watch for the morning,
> more than those who watch for the morning.
> O Israel, hope in the Lord!
> For with the Lord there is steadfast love,
> and with him is great power to redeem.
> It is he who will redeem Israel from all its iniquities.

And from 1 Timothy 1: 'Now to the King eternal, immortal, invisible, the only God, be honour and glory for ever and ever. Amen.'
Thank you.

THE 2014 HOUSE OF BISHOPS' DECLARATION ON THE MINISTRY OF BISHOPS AND PRIESTS

An excerpt from General Synod Paper GS Misc 1076 (See Chapter 4)

Introduction

1. The character and calling of the Church of England are set out in the Preface to the Declaration of Assent, which all clergy are required to make at ordination and subsequently on admission to any office. As part of the One, Holy, Catholic and Apostolic Church it is called to proclaim afresh in each generation the faith uniquely revealed in the Holy Scriptures and set forth in the catholic creeds.

2. Those who serve the Church of England in holy orders are required to affirm their loyalty to this 'inheritance of faith' and bring 'the grace and truth of Christ to this generation.' Bishops have a particular responsibility to gather God's people and build up the Body of Christ. We have each promised at our consecration to promote peace and reconciliation in the Church and to seek to unite its members in a holy fellowship of truth and love.

3. The opening of all orders of ministry equally to women and men is a significant moment in the long history of this part of the Church Catholic. It brings with it new opportunities for building up the Body of Christ and proclaiming the good news of the kingdom.

4. It also brings with it a particular responsibility for us, as a House of Bishops. As well as seeking to channel and nurture the energy and renewal that will flow from this development we have a duty to ensure that the welfare of the whole Church of England is sustained in all its theological depth and breadth. We accordingly commend this declaration to all members of the Church of England so that the good gifts that God has given to all His people may be used to His glory.

Statement of guiding principles

5. The House reaffirms the five guiding principles which it first commended in May 2013 when submitting legislative proposals to the General Synod for the consecration of women to the episcopate and which the Synod welcomed in its resolution of 20 November 2013. They need to be read one with the other and held together in tension, rather than being applied selectively:

   a. Now that legislation has been passed to enable women to become bishops the Church of England is fully and unequivocally committed to all orders of ministry being open equally to all, without reference to gender, and holds that those whom it has duly ordained and appointed to office are the true and lawful holders of the office which they occupy and thus deserve due respect and canonical obedience;

   b. Anyone who ministers within the Church of England must be prepared to acknowledge that the Church of England has reached a clear decision on the matter;

   c. Since it continues to share the historic episcopate with other Churches, including the Roman Catholic Church, the

Orthodox Church and those provinces of the Anglican Communion which continue to ordain only men as priests or bishops, the Church of England acknowledges that its own clear decision on ministry and gender is set within a broader process of discernment within the Anglican Communion and the whole Church of God;

d. Since those within the Church of England who, on grounds of theological conviction, are unable to receive the ministry of women bishops or priests continue to be within the spectrum of teaching and tradition of the Anglican Communion, the Church of England remains committed to enabling them to flourish within its life and structures; and

e. Pastoral and sacramental provision for the minority within the Church of England will be made without specifying a limit of time and in a way that maintains the highest possible degree of communion and contributes to mutual flourishing across the whole Church of England.

Statement on the announcement of my appointment, April 2017 (See Chapter 6)

Friends, it is very good indeed to be with you. Thank you for being here. These are unusual circumstances, to say the least, and not circumstances any of us would have chosen. Clearly, the events which have led up to today do not reflect well on any part of the Church of England.

So let me begin by paying tribute to Bishop Philip North: to his whole-hearted commitment to the poor, and his prayerfulness, and especially to the generous and courageous decision he took to withdraw from his nomination to this post in the interests of the unity of the church.

Secondly I want to acknowledge the work which must follow when the inquiry led by Sir Philip Mawer is complete, if we are to recover confidence in the concept of mutual flourishing and in the five guiding principles as the best tool presently available for achieving it. I remain fully committed to them, although I am also certain there will be lessons to be learned not just for us here, in the Diocese of Sheffield, but for the whole Church of England. In fact, I believe that for some of those lessons the wider church will have cause to be grateful to this diocese and I want to honour that.

Thirdly, I'd like to thank Bishop Peter and all the people of this diocese, lay and ordained, for the work you've already done in recent weeks to heal the wounds which had been exposed by Bishop Philip's nomination, and later by his withdrawal. The work of healing and reconciliation is well underway and I look forward to sharing in that process with you (and not least with Dr Sarah Hills and the diocesan senior staff) as a matter of urgency over the coming months.

Next week is Holy Week; a week today it will be Good Friday. There is no better time for followers of Jesus, within this diocese and beyond it, to gather in penitence and faith at the foot of the cross, where the Lord calls us to find in him not only forgiveness and peace but a fresh commissioning to take the good news of his saving death and glorious resurrection to a needy world.

So I am drawn afresh, and I want to draw you also, to Christ and to him crucified; and in this moment of pain and hope, there are three things I want to say about myself and about my own sense of calling as I stand here today.

I want to share with you, to start with, the time when, as a 13-year-old, I was first conscious of the call of Jesus. I grew up in a Christian home, but the defining experience of my life came when I was a young teenager and sensed that God was inviting me to commit to the adventure of following Jesus. I chose to respond with my whole self and it was the best decision I have ever made. I share that with you because I am here this morning not primarily as your Bishop-designate, but as a disciple of Jesus, seeking to live out, each day, a life worthy of my baptism.

But I also refer to that experience because such a high proportion of those who make lasting commitments to Jesus do so as I did – as teenagers. Of course, the Church of God is called to proclaim the good news to all people at all times and in all places, but I am so encouraged to see in the current priorities of the Diocese of Sheffield a commitment to reach out to that age group in particular and you can be sure I will do everything I can to make that outreach fruitful. And that is just one part of the Diocesan Strategy which energises me: so much of it (from 'Growing the body of Christ' to 'A little letter on Giving', from 'Salt and Light' to 'Forming and equipping the people of God') expresses what I firmly believe. So the direction of travel for the diocese will remain unchanged; I can assure you there will be no sudden lurch to a new set of priorities.

The second thing I want to mention is the publication of the Faith in the City report in 1985. Some of you will remember it. It came out while I was training for the ordained ministry and it's a document which has profoundly shaped my own sense of calling. It is no coincidence that I come to you from Liverpool: a northern, urban city with a northern, urban cathedral; a cathedral with a food bank and an employability programme; a cathedral which seeks to give a voice to the poor. And it's no coincidence that we are meeting here, in a place where the church has engaged to such good effect with the local community, proclaiming the kingdom of God by addressing the challenges and celebrating the opportunities of this place, liberating its neglected assets and blessing its unfulfilled potential. The gospel of Jesus Christ confronts social and economic inequalities, and we see here here a great example of how transformative the church can be; and I'm looking forward to visiting similar examples of kingdom partnership in Rotherham and Doncaster later today.

But the difficulties facing our most deprived communities (and therefore the church congregations in our most deprived communities) are not going to go away in the course of the next decade, and helping to address those issues will be another key priority for me.

Finally, I want to say a word about how these past four months have been for me, personally. No one I've spoken to has been able to think of any other occasion when a newly announced diocesan bishop has been, as a matter of public record, not the first choice. You might be wondering how that feels. And my honest answer is, it feels fine, actually. When I was invited by the Crown Nominations Commission, to explore the possibility of a call to Sheffield last autumn I was thrilled. As I read the statement of need produced by the Diocese there seemed to me to be a fit to my gifts and experience. And it's true that I was pretty devastated when the news came before Christmas that I was not the preferred candidate. At that point I did what any Christian would do: I tried to resign myself to the apparent will of God and move on. For three months that was my daily prayer – but I never managed it. Throughout the first three months of this year, I never managed to shake off the thought of Sheffield. The closest I got was to be reconciled to… never being fully reconciled. So this appointment was never second choice to me.

At times I have found the past few months quite gruelling – but in that respect I know very well that I am by no means the only one! In my case, perhaps (in the providence of God) the process has tempered me, as steel is tempered. In all the 30 years of my ordained ministry, however, it has been vital for me to know that I am where the Lord has called me to be – and I definitely have that conviction here, and now.

This is not a diocese I know well. So there is a great deal for me to learn, from you and from all my sisters and brothers in ministry and mission here. Over the course of the last 30 years, I've got to know and love the north east, the west Midlands and Merseyside, and now I shall have the great privilege of getting to know and love South Yorkshire and the East Riding too. There is much in what I have already discovered which excites and inspires me; but I am also aware how much there is for us to do together in the service of Christ. I am hugely looking forward to the task before us and will give myself to it without reservation, in partnership with you all. Thank you.

Sermon preached at the Service of Installation, September 2017 (See Chapter 11)

2 Corinthians 8.1-9: Grace, gratitude and generosity

Introduction

Let me begin, if I may, with some thanks. Cathy and I are hugely grateful for the warmth of the welcome we've received since we moved into Bishopscroft in June. We have very quickly been made to feel at home and among friends, here at the Cathedral and across the Diocese, here in this city and across the region. I've been particularly grateful for the warmth of welcome I've experienced this past week, as I've walked from one extremity of the Diocese (almost the farthest point from this Cathedral Church) to this place. If you didn't know, that's basically what I've been doing this past week, Monday to Friday. I've covered over 50 miles on foot, passing through 8 of the 12 deaneries of the Diocese and 25 of its 175 parishes. And if my itinerary didn't take in your deanery this week, don't worry (or, for that matter, don't breathe a sigh of relief just yet) – I hope to put my walking boots on again soon to complete the set. Where I have been this week I've been moved by the reception I've received and I mean it when I say that Cathy and I are really glad to be here and are very much looking forward to getting to know you and to working alongside you in the mission to which God is calling us together, for the sake of the Gospel and of his coming kingdom. We are grateful not least for all the assurances we have received of people's prayers and we do urge you please not to stop praying for us any time soon!

It is 15 months since the farewell service took place here, to mark the conclusion of Bishop Steven's ministry in this diocese and obviously this is not the time to rehearse all that has taken place since then. But almost no one here will be unaware of the heavy burden which has been borne during that time by the members of the bishop's staff and above all by Bishop Peter in his role as acting bishop and I wonder if I could ask you please to take this moment to express your appreciation to the bishop's staff in general but especially, and very particularly, to Bishop Peter.

I also want to thank Dean Peter, Canons Chris and Keith and all the Cathedral staff and volunteers for the arrangements you've put in place for today. Thank you too to those of you who've come to support Cathy and me from farther afield: it means a great deal to us to have you here – friends not only from Liverpool, but from Lichfield and Walsall, from Gateshead, Oxford and Teesside, from Durham and Worksop. Do join us over at the Cutler's Hall after the service if you can: we would love to greet as many of you in person as possible.

And finally, I'd like to thank Sky television. Sky has no interest at all in this occasion, of course; but when the current Championship fixture list was published in July, after we'd agreed this date for the installation, it showed that the first Sheffield derby of the season was also scheduled for this afternoon. So, somewhat reluctantly, we moved this service to tomorrow – only for Sky to nominate the derby match for live broadcast, so moving it to tomorrow and freeing up our original first choice slot for this service. The fact that the match now conflicts with the Sheffield 10k road race, also scheduled for tomorrow, is, thankfully, somebody else's headache. The Lord works in mysterious ways.

Now, for the next ten minutes I want to turn my attention to those verses from 2 Corinthians 8 which Heidi read for us a few moments ago. In the process I want to speak to you about Jesus, the grace of

God and generosity. Jesus, grace and generosity. This is not the last time you will hear me place the emphasis there. In fact, though I hope never to bore you, I do expect to become predictable in the way I return again and again to just this: Jesus, grace and generosity.

Jesus

Jesus, then, first of all. The only explicit reference to Jesus in our reading comes right at the end, climactically – so at the risk of offending fans of The Sound of Music, who will doubtless feel that I ought to begin at the very beginning, I suggest that on this occasion the final verse of our reading is the very best place to start. 'You know the generous act of our Lord Jesus Christ, that though he was rich, yet for your sakes he became poor, so that by his poverty, you might become rich.'

At the heart of the Christian gospel is a transaction, an exchange, by which every individual believer is transformed because of what Jesus has done. This, ultimately, is what we Christians mean when we talk about Jesus as our saviour. Once we were lost, but now in Christ we are found; once we were blind, but now in Christ we see; once we were hurt, but now in Christ we are made whole; once we were dead, but now in Christ we are alive again; once we were bound, but now in Christ we are set free; once we were poor, but now because of Jesus, we are rich.

The focal point of that transaction and exchange is the cross, on which Jesus died as our Saviour, but from which God raised him from the dead; the cross through which at the cost of his own life Jesus won for us the salvation he now calls us to hold out to the world.

But here's the thing: where our English translation says, 'You know the generous act of our Lord Jesus Christ,' the original Greek text says,

'You know the grace of our Lord Jesus Christ.' What Jesus did so generously, he did by grace, he did as grace: he offered himself for our salvation as an act of grace, to manifest fully and finally the unmerited favour of God. He did it as something utterly undeserved by us, as sheer gift.

Grace and generosity

Having said something first of all about Jesus, then, let me say something further about grace and generosity.

I wonder when was the last time you received a gift which you knew in your heart to be undeserved? Perhaps it was also unexpected. To touch you, it need not necessarily have been an expensive gift. Most of us know what it's like to be disarmed by an inexpensive gift from a child or by the spontaneous kindness of a stranger. If you can call to mind a gift you've received, whether recently or long ago, that you know to have been unmerited, undeserved, you'll also be aware of the effect that gift had on you, on your heart – you'll be aware of your gratitude. Thankfulness is the only proper response to a gift. Gratitude is the only proper response to grace.

And so it is in the Christian life. Those who truly experience the grace of God, who recognise it and embrace it, are bound to be thankful. I'd go as far as to say that gratitude is a characteristic mark of authentic Christian faith, in every authentic Christian disciple, in every authentic Christian community. When that is not there, something vital has been lost, some grasp of the grace of God has been lost. At least, this seems to me to be Paul's argument in the passage Heidi read for us. Paul expects those who have experienced grace to practise it – those who've experienced the unmerited favour of God to extend unmerited favour to others, those who've experienced the undeserved generosity of God to live generously as a result. Generosity is the way grace works itself out in and through the lives of Christians and Christian churches: it's in our DNA because Jesus puts it there.

So take a look at the earlier 2 paragraphs, the first 8 verses of our reading, on page 19 of your service booklet. First, in the opening verses, Paul points out that the grace of God which has been granted to the churches of Macedonia, to the Philippians, for example, and the Thessalonians, has changed them. It has overflowed in a wealth of generosity on their part. That's what the grace of God does: it generates generosity. Or take verse 5: because of what they were given, they gave themselves – they gave themselves to the Lord and to Paul and his companions. Those who receive the gift of grace can't help but give in response.

And so in verses 7 to 8, Paul urges the Corinthians to live up to their calling. Since they too have received grace, he is looking for their gratitude. You'll see that at the end of verse 7 Paul urges the Corinthians, who excel in so much, to excel in what our English version calls 'this generous undertaking' (in fact the same phrase occurs at the end of verse 6 too). But the Greek text is simply this: 'just as you overflow (it's the same word he used in speaking of the generosity of the Macedonians in verse 2) 'just as you overflow in everything, overflow also in grace.' The phrase 'This generous undertaking' simply translates the word 'grace': 'since you have received abundant grace,' Paul urges here, 'overflow with grace.' Let the grace you've received transform you, let it generate in you abundant generosity. Let it do its proper work: as you have freely received, freely give.

Generosity and grace today

Which begs the question, what does this mean for you and me here today, and for the Diocese of Sheffield in the coming years? It's with those questions that I want to finish.

You see, insofar as I have any sense yet of what the Lord has called me here for (as your new bishop), it is to foster generosity, to call us all back, again and again, to the grace which God has made known in the face of Jesus Christ and to the gratitude, expressed as generosity, which is the only fitting response to that grace. I believe the Lord is calling us, as a diocese, to be generous with Jesus.

And by those three words, 'generous with Jesus,' I mean two things. I mean, first of all, that those who align with Jesus are bound to be generous as he is generous. We are bound to be generous, both in the sense that an obligation has been placed upon us and in the sense that the spirit of God, the spirit of grace, will (truly will) form generosity in us. It's bound to happen.

One of the striking things about our Bible reading is the fact that what Paul had immediately in mind when he wrote to the Corinthians in these terms was a collection: a collection he was organising among the mostly Gentile churches in Greece, to relieve the needs of the mostly Jewish churches in Jerusalem and Judea. I say it's one of the striking things, because Paul never once mentions money in the whole of 2 Corinthians 8 and 9. A generous donation to a charitable cause might have been his principal aim – but to get there, he holds fast to the language of grace and gratitude.

Now it's true that shortly we will be singing a hymn during which a collection will be taken. And of course I hope you will give generously – of course I do. The generosity of Christians is rightly expressed in the way we use our money – and there will certainly be times in the days to come when you hear me calling for financial generosity. But the generosity to which you and I are called, as we seek to express our gratitude for the grace which has touched our lives, can never be confined to the way we use our money. No: our calling is to live generously, period. Our calling is to think generous thoughts, to speak generous words, to act generously in every way. You might well contribute generously when the collection plate comes around, but my friends, that won't get you off the hook. If you have experienced the grace of God, your calling is to give yourself in response – and that will be manifest not least in the way in which you relate to other people, and especially those who differ from you. Your challenge, under God, is to deal generously with them. And it's not enough simply to respond generously when others are generous to you: if you belong to Jesus, you are called to set the standard. That, by the way, is one reason I am so grateful for the tone, as well as for the content, of the Mawer report published just over a week ago. It sets a generous standard.

So that's the first thing I mean when I say I believe God is calling us as a diocese to be generous with Jesus: as those who are with Jesus we are bound to be generous as he is generous. But my final point is this: when I speak of being generous with Jesus, I also mean secondly that in seeking, as Christians and as Christian communities, to be generous, we will want to be generous not least with the Lord Jesus himself: we will want to share him. We will want to be generous with Jesus in that sense too.

In other words, there's an evangelistic challenge here: a generous church is a missionary church. We can't help ourselves: those of us who have received Christ freely, can't help but give Christ freely away. We long for others to unite their voices with ours, in testimony to what the Lord has done for them. We long for them to say: 'Once we were lost, but now in Christ we are found; once we were blind, but now in Christ we see; once we were wounded, but now in Christ we are made whole; once we were dead, but now in Christ we are alive again; once we were bound, but now in Christ we are set free; once we were poor, but now because of Jesus, we are rich.'

Conclusion

It is this sort of church that I believe the Lord has called me to assist in fostering, here in this Diocese, in the next phase of our life: a church marked out by generosity; a church full of gratitude; a church which, day in and day out, is shaped by its experience of God's grace; a church in which, day after day, the grace of God generates in us an overflowing generosity; a church which is therefore generous with the Gospel, and generous in its behaviour and above all in the way it relates across difference. Nothing less than a diocese which is generous with Jesus is worthy of the grace which God the Father has lavished upon us, through the Spirit, in Jesus Christ our Lord. Amen.

www.ingramcontent.com/pod-product-compliance
Lightning Source LLC
Chambersburg PA
CBHW020539080526
44583CB00013B/915